11+ Non-verbal Reasoning

WORKBOOK 1

Non-verbal Reasoning Technique

Dr Stephen C Curran
with Andrea Richardson

Edited by Katrina MacKay

This book belongs to

Accelerated Education Publications Ltd

Contents

Pages

1. Elements

1. Shapes — 3-7
2. Fills — 8-11
3. Lines — 12-15
4. Key Questions used in Non-verbal Reasoning — 16-19

2. Movements

1. Reflection — 20-22
2. Rotation — 23-25
3. Superimposition — 26-28
4. Transposition — 29-31

3. Manipulations

1. Size — 32-34
2. Addition — 35-37
3. Subtraction — 38-40
4. Frequency (Counting) — 41-43

4. Patterns

1. Repetition — 44-46
2. Cumulation — 47-49

5. Layering

1. Level One — 50-52
2. Level Two — 53-55
3. Level Three — 56-58

© 2015 Stephen Curran

Chapter One
ELEMENTS

Non-verbal Reasoning questions combine three **Elements**:
Shapes • Fills • Lines

1. Shapes
a. Standard Palette

This comprises all 'closed' geometrically defined shapes.
Triangles • Quadrilaterals • Polygons • Circles

(i) Triangles

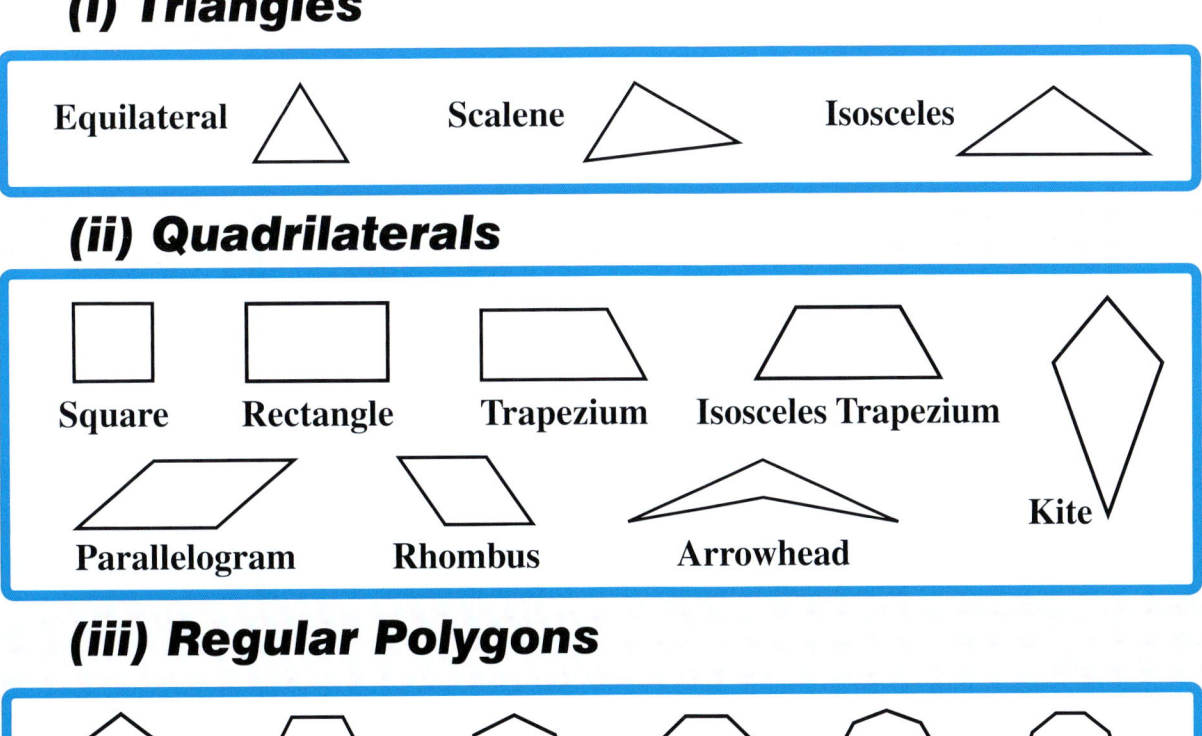

(ii) Quadrilaterals

(iii) Regular Polygons

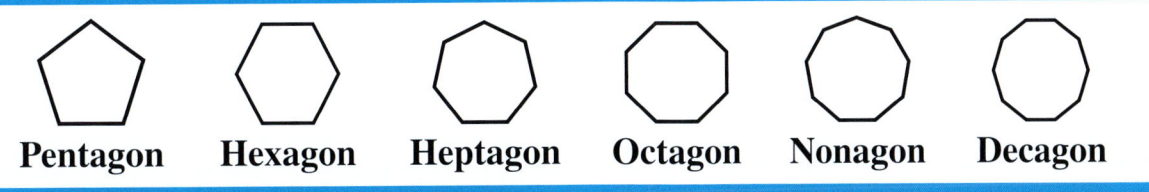

(iv) Circular Shapes

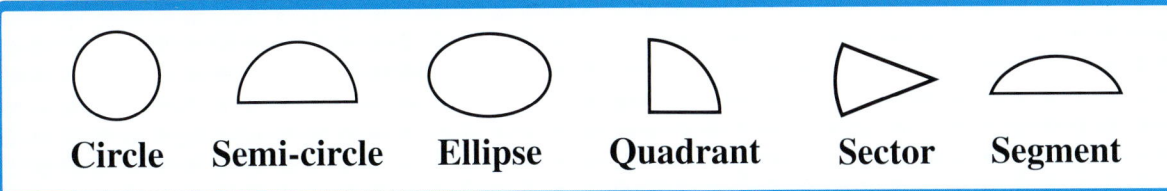

© 2015 Stephen Curran

(v) Irregular Polygons

Irregular shapes have unequal sides and angles.

General Quadrilateral   Pentagon   Hexagon

b. Specialist Palette

This comprises everyday recognisable 'closed' shapes.

Straight Shapes • Curved Shapes

Other shapes could be shown that are not in these palettes.

(i) Straight Shapes

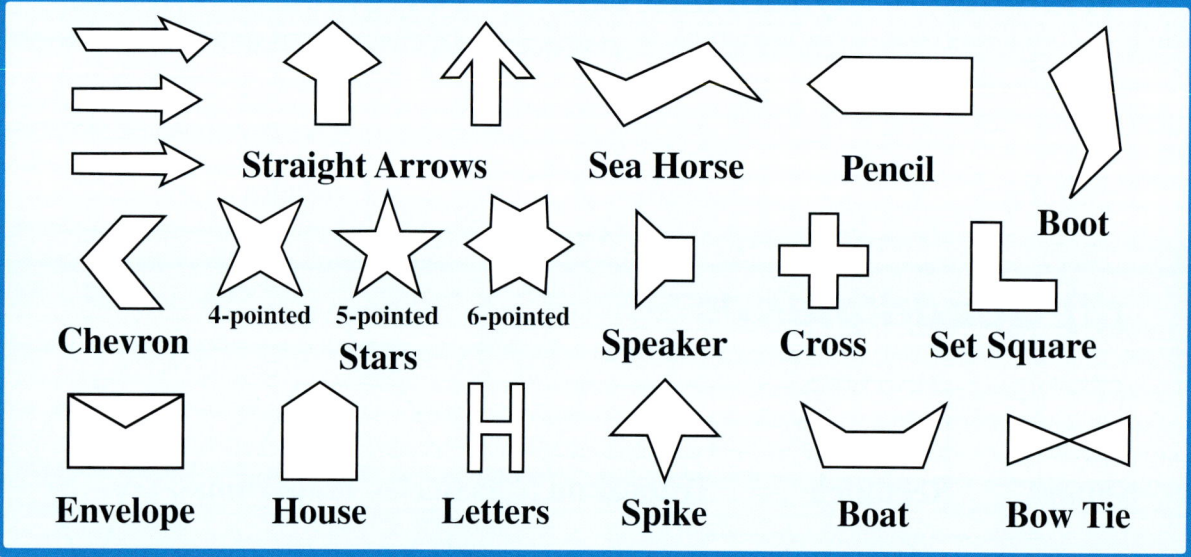

(ii) Curved Shapes

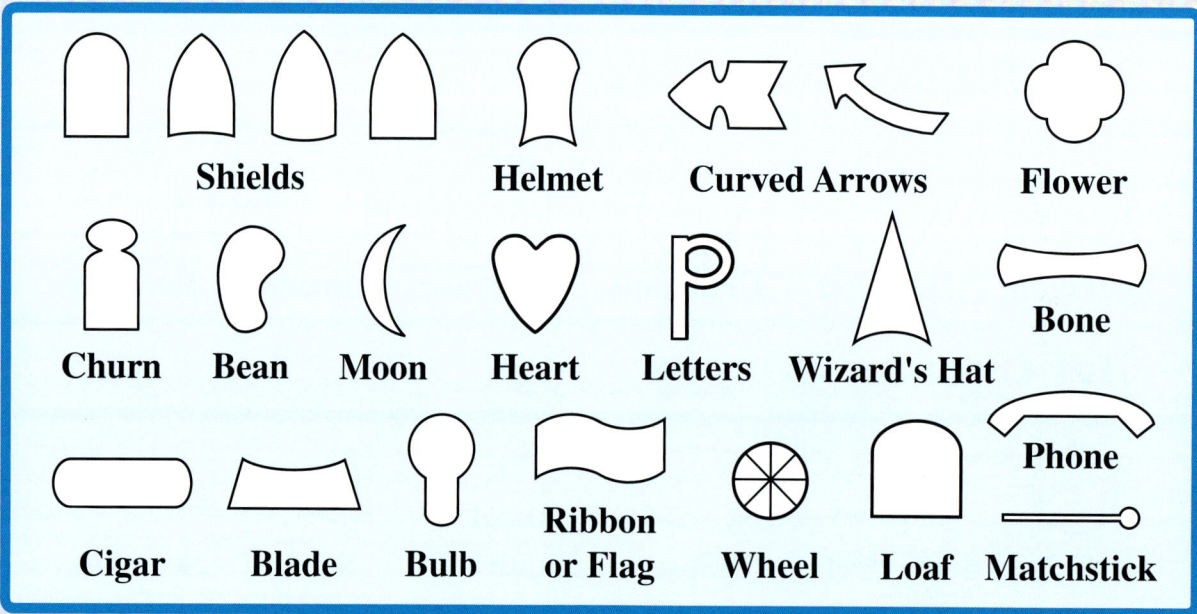

c. Naming Shapes

It is important in Non-verbal Reasoning questions to be able to identify and give **Names to Shapes**. It is much easier to describe what is happening to a shape if it is given a name.

(i) Standard Shapes

Exercise 1: 1   Name the following shapes:

1)   2) 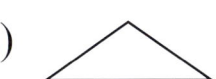   3) 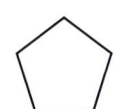   4)

5) 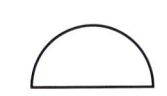   6) 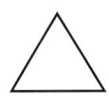   7) 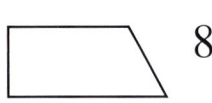   8)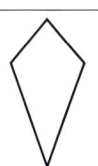

9)    10)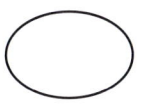

 Record scores out of ten here

(ii) Specialist Shapes

Exercise 1: 2   Name the following shapes:

1) 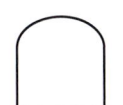   2)    3) 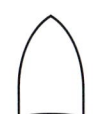   4)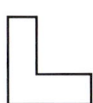

5)    6)    7) 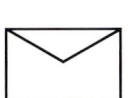   8)

9)   10)

 Score

© 2015 Stephen Curran

d. Shape Questions

Exercise 1: 3   Answer the following:

1) Which is the next shape in the series?

△ □ ⬠ ⬡ ?   a ⬡ b ⬡ c ⌂ d ○

Answer ____ This shape is called a(n) _____.

2) Which shape does not fit in with the others?

a   b   c   d   e

Answer ____ This shape is called a(n) _____.

3) Which shape belongs to this family of shapes?

a   b   c   d

Answer ____ This shape is called a(n) _____.

4) Which shape is most like the Test Shape?

Test Shape   a   b   c   d   e

Answer ____ This shape is called a(n) _____.

5) Which shape is the odd one out?

a   b   c   d   e

Answer ____

This shape is called a(n) _____.

6) Which shape does not fit in with these shapes?

    a   b   c   d   e

Answer ____   This shape is called a(n) _____.

7) Which shape belongs to this family of shapes?

Answer ____   This shape is called a(n) _____.

8) Which shape does not fit in with the others?

    a   b   c   d   e

Answer ____   This shape is called a(n) _____.

9) Which is the next shape in the series?

Answer ____   This shape is called a(n) _____.

10) Which shape does not fit in with the other shapes?

    a   b   c   d   e

Answer ____   This shape is called a(n) _____.   Score ____

© 2015 Stephen Curran

2. Fills
a. Fill Categories

'Closed' shape **Fills** comprise five different categories:
Block • Shaded • Cross-hatched • Liquid • Dotted

b. Fill Palette
(i) Block Fills

Black  Grey  White

(ii) Shaded Fills

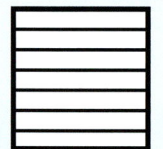  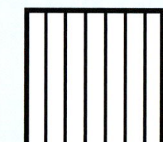 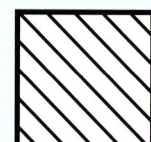

Horizontal Solid Line • Right Slant Solid Line • Vertical Solid Line • Left Slant Solid Line

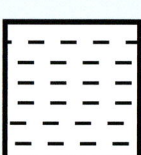  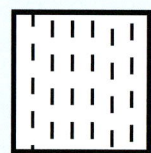 

Horizontal Dashed Line • Right Slant Dashed Line • Vertical Dashed Line • Left Slant Dashed Line

(iii) Cross-hatched Fills

Squares 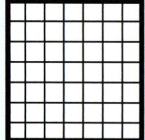   Lattice

(iv) Liquid Fills

 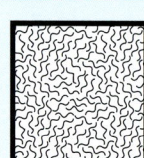

Speckled • Mottled

(v) Dotted Fills

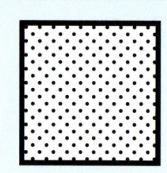 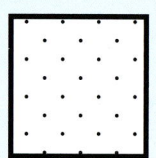

Close • Spaced

c. Naming Fills

Giving **Names to Fills** also helps when describing shapes.

Exercise 1: 4   Name the following fills:

1)

Fill category: __Liquid__
Fill type: _____

2)

Fill category: _____
Fill type: __Vertical Dashed__

3)

Fill category: _____
Fill type: _____

4)

Fill category: _____
Fill type: _____

5)

Fill category: _____
Fill type: _____

6)

Fill category: _____
Fill type: _____

7)

Fill category: _____
Fill type: _____

8)

Fill category: _____
Fill type: _____

9)

Fill category: _____
Fill type: _____

10)

Fill category: _____
Fill type: _____

Score

d. Fill Questions

Exercise 1: 5   Answer the following:

1) Which shape is next in the series?

    ?   a   b   c   d

   Answer ____
   Fill category: _____ Fill type: _____

2) Which shape does not fit in with the others?

   Answer ____   a   b   c   d   e
   Fill category: _____ Fill type: _____

3) Which shape is next in the series?

    ?   a   b   c   d

   Answer ____
   Fill category: _____ Fill type: _____

4) Which shape does not fit in with the others?

   Answer ____   a   b   c   d   e
   Fill category: _____ Fill type: _____

5) Which shape is next in the series?

    ?   a   b   c   d

   Answer ____
   Fill category: _____ Fill type: _____

© 2015 Stephen Curran

6) Which two shapes are most alike?

Answer ___ and ___   a   b   c   d   e

Fill category: _____ Fill type: _____

7) Which shape is the odd one out?

Answer ___   a   b   c   d   e

Fill category: _____ Fill type: _____

8) Which shape is most like the Test Shape?

Test Shape   a   b   c   d   e

Fill category: _____

Answer ___   Fill type: _____

9) Which is the next shape in the series?

Answer ___   a   b   c   d

Fill category: _____ Fill type: _____

10) Which shape is most like the Test Shape?

Test Shape   a   b   c   d   e

Answer ___
Fill category: _____
Fill type: _____

Score ___

© 2015 Stephen Curran

3. Lines
a. Line Palette

All **Line Types** have three main properties:	1. Solid — Dashed - - - Dotted ·····
	2. Straight — — — Curved ⌒
	3. Thin —— Thick ━━

Example: This line type is described as: ⁀(dotted curve)⁀ — Dotted, Curved, Thick

b. Line Shape Palette

This comprises everyday recognisable 'open' **Line Shapes**.
Straight Line Shapes • **Curved Line Shapes**
This palette is not exhaustive as other shapes also exist.

(i) Straight Line Shapes

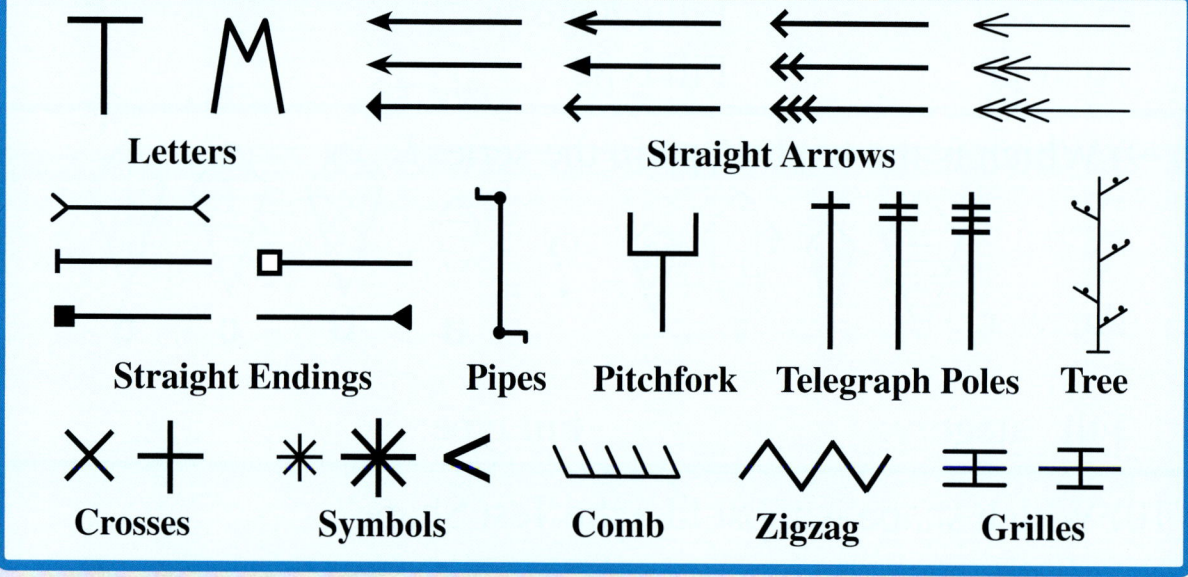

Letters • Straight Arrows

Straight Endings • Pipes • Pitchfork • Telegraph Poles • Tree

Crosses • Symbols • Comb • Zigzag • Grilles

(ii) Curved Line Shapes

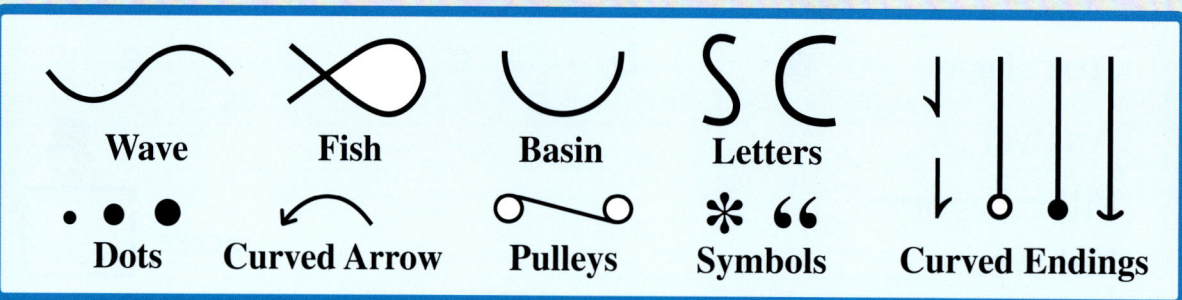

Wave • Fish • Basin • Letters

Dots • Curved Arrow • Pulleys • Symbols • Curved Endings

c. Naming Lines

> **Naming Lines** and Line Shapes helps with identification.

(i) Straight Line Shapes

Exercise 1: 6a   Identify the following line types:

1)
Type: _Dotted_ _Straight_ _Thick_
Shape: _____

2)
Type: _____ _____ _____
Shape: _Cross_

3)
Type: _____ _____ _____
Shape: _____

4)
Type: _____ _____ _____
Shape: _____

5)
Type: _____ _____ _____
Shape: _____

(ii) Curved Line Shapes

Exercise 1: 6b   Identify the following line types:

6)
Type: _____ _____ _____
Shape: _____

7)
Type: _____ _____ _____
Shape: _____

8)
Type: _____ _____ _____
Shape: _____

9)
Type: _____ _____ _____
Shape: _____

10)
Type: _____ _____ _____
Shape: _____

Score

d. Line Questions

Exercise 1: 7   Answer the following:

1) Which is the next figure in the series?

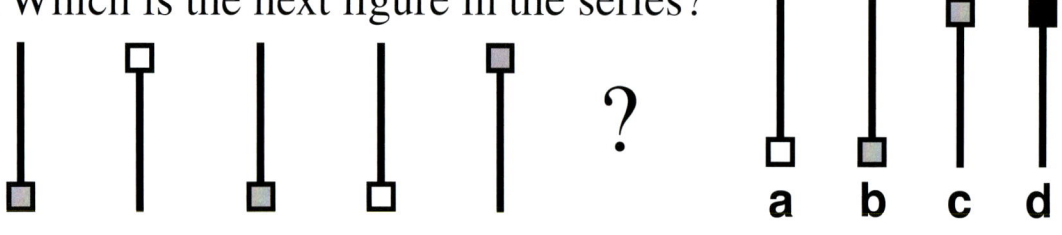

Answer ____   These figures have _____ endings.

2) Which figure does not fit in with the others?

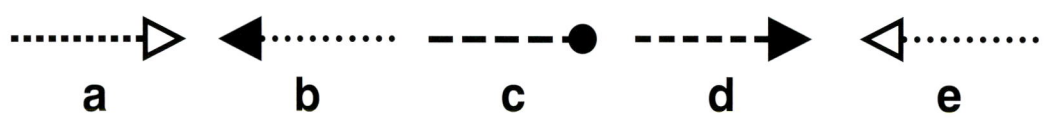

Answer ____   This figure has a _____ ending.

3) Which figure belongs to this family of figures?

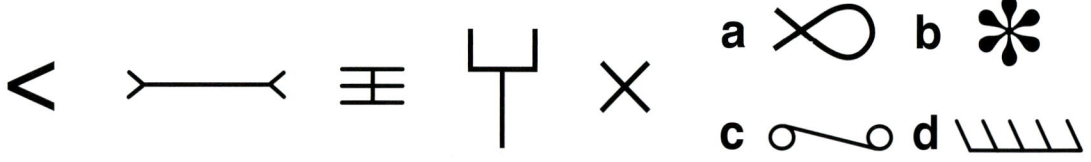

Answer ____   This figure is called a(n) _____.

4) Which figure is most like the Test Figure?

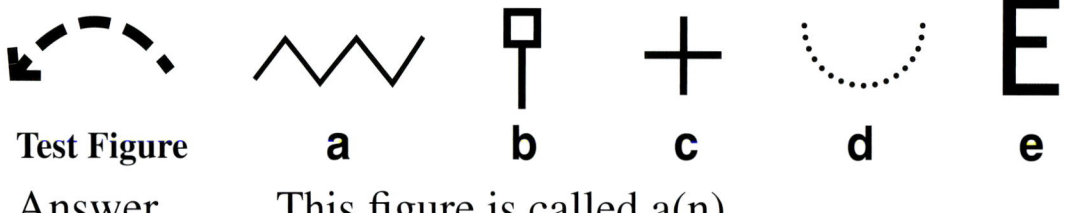

Answer ____   This figure is called a(n) _____.

5) Which figure is the odd one out?

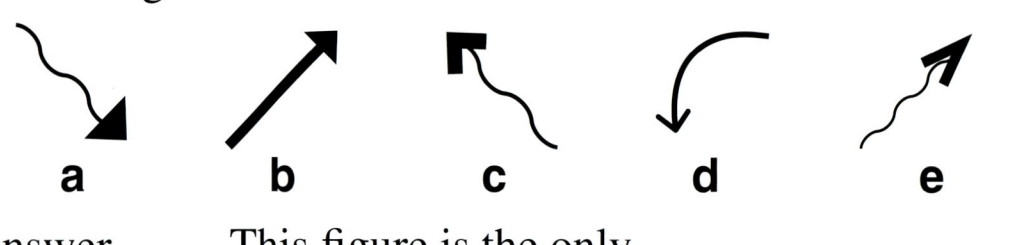

Answer ____   This figure is the only _____.

6) Which figure does not fit in with the other figures?

a   b   c   d   e

Answer ____   This line type is: ____ ____ ____

7) Which figure belongs to this family of figures?

a   b
c   d

Answer ____   This line type is: ____ ____ ____

8) Which figure does not fit in with the others?

a   b   c   d   e

Answer ____   This line type is: ____ ____ ____

9) Which figure is next in the series?

∧ > ∨ < ?

a ∧   b >
c ∧   d ∨

Answer ____   These figures are Straight _____.

10) Which figure belongs to this family of figures?

P G B J U D

a T   b R
c X   d L

Answer ____
The line type is:
____ ____ ____

Score ____

4. Key Questions used in Non-verbal Reasoning

All Non-verbal Reasoning questions are centred around just three key areas. It is important to be able to identify:

Similarity • Difference • Pattern

These questions have already been used in this book:
1) Which shape is most similar to the shape given?
2) Which shape is most different from the shape given?
3) Which shape is the next shape in the series?

a. Similarity

Shapes are **Similar** if they are like each other in some way. This likeness can apply to any aspect of the shape or shapes.

These two shapes are identical, except they are of a different size and fill type. The second shape has also been rotated 45° in a Clockwise direction in relation to the first shape.

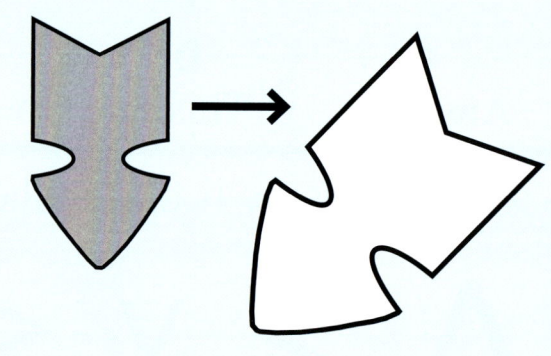

Similarity involves identifying one or more common characteristics between shapes.

Example: Which shape is most similar to the Test Shape?

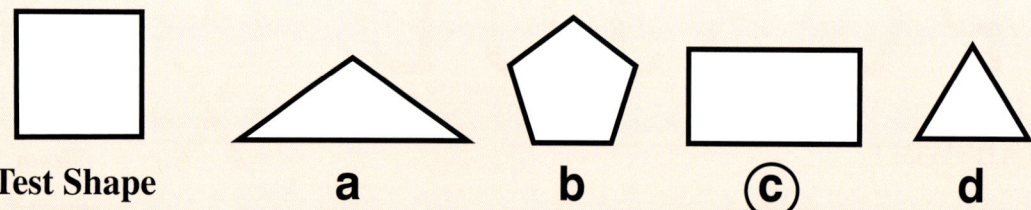

Answer: Shape **c** is most similar as it has four sides.

b. Difference

Shapes are **Different** if they are unlike each other in some way. Difference can mean the shape or shapes have no likeness at all, or there are one or more aspects not alike.

Both these shapes are Stars with the same fill type but they have a different number of sides.

Difference involves spotting the shape most unlike the rest.

Example: Which shape is different from the other shapes?

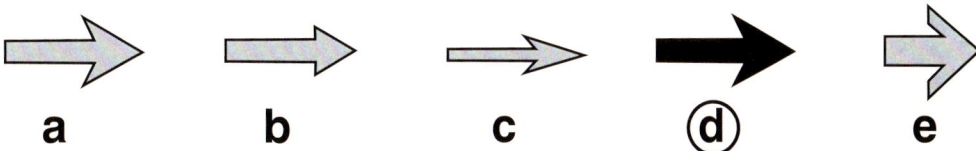

    a   b   c   ⓓ   e

Answer: Shape **d** is different because it has a Black Fill.

c. Pattern

A **Repetitive** or **Cumulative Pattern** can be established in a series or sequence of shapes or figures (see pages 44-49).

The fill changes from Grey to White to Grey repetitively. One more Circle with a Black Fill is added each time cumulatively.

    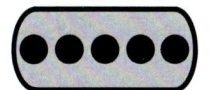

A pattern is identified by spotting repetition or cumulation.

Example: Which shape is next in the series?

   ?   a   b

Answer: Shape **c** is next because it is bigger and it has a White Fill.

ⓒ   d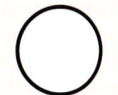

Exercise 1: 8   Answer the following:

1) Which is the next shape in the series?

Answer ____   Why? _____

2) Which shape does not fit in with the others?

Answer ____   Why not? _____

3) Which shape is next in the series?

Answer ____   Why? _____

4) Which shape does not fit in with the others?

Answer ____   Why not? _____

5) Which is the next shape in the series?

Answer ____   Why? _____

6) Which two shapes are most alike?

a   b   c   d   e

Answer ____ and ____   Why? _____

7) Which shape is the odd one out?

a   b   c   d   e

Answer ____   Why? _____

8) Which shape is most similar to the Test Shape?

Test Shape   a   b   c   d   e

Answer ____   Why? _____

9) Which shape is next in the series?

a   b   c   d

Answer ____   Why? _____

10) Which shape is most like the Test Shape?

Test Shape   a   b   c   d   e

Score

Answer ____   Why? _____

Chapter Two
MOVEMENTS

In Non-verbal Reasoning, shapes can **Move** in four ways:
Reflection • Rotation • Superimposition • Transposition

1. Reflection

A shape can be **Reflected** across an imaginary Mirror Line or Line of Reflection. Shape **A** is reflected the other side of the Mirror Line to form shape **B**.

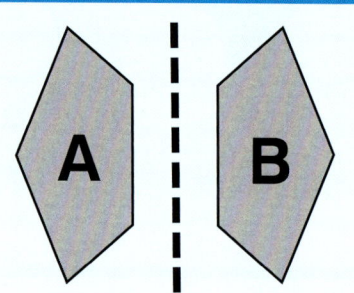

Key Non-verbal Reasoning questions apply to reflections:

Example 1: Which shape is a reflection of the Test Shape?

Test Shape   a   b   ⓒ   d   e

Answer: **c** is a reflection of the Test Shape.

Example 2: Which pair of shapes are not reflections?

a   ⓑ   c   d

Answer: **b** - The Slanted Shaded Fills are not reflections.

Example 3: Which is the next shape in the series?

?   a   b   ⓒ   d

Answer: **c** - The Shape reflects correctly and has the correct Liquid Fill type.

Exercise 2: 1   Answer the following:

1) Which is the next shape in the series?

Answer ____   Fill category: _____
Fill type: _____

2) Which pair of shapes does not fit in with the others?

Answer ____   These Shapes are called _____ .

3) Which is the next figure in the series?

Answer ____   Fill category: _____
Fill type: _____

4) Which figure does not fit in with the others?

Why not? _____
Answer ____   _____

5) Which letter is next in the series?

Q R S Z B F G ?   a M   b J   c A   d L

Answer ____   Why? _____
_____

6) Which two pairs of shapes are most alike?

a   b   c   d   e

Answer ____ and ____   Why? _____

7) Which pair of shapes is the odd one out?

a   b   c   d   e

Answer ____   i) Why? _____
ii) These shapes are called _____.

8) Which figure is a reflection of the Test Figure?

Test Figure   a   b   c   d   e

Answer ____   The inner shape is called a(n) _____.

9) Which is the next shape in the series?

?   a   b   c   d

What is this shape called?

Answer ____   _____

10) Which figure is a reflection of the Test Figure?

Test Figure   a   b   c   d   e

Answer ____   The outer shape is called a(n) _____.

Score

2. Rotation

In Non-verbal Reasoning, shapes can **Rotate** in a Clockwise or Anticlockwise direction.

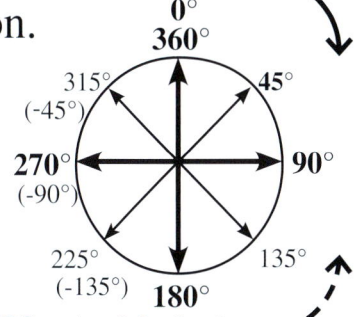

To avoid confusion it is best to measure the rotation by the shortest route. This will be in either a **Clockwise** or an **Anticlockwise** direction around the **360°** turn. There are three main rotations:

45°($\frac{1}{8}$) turn   90°($\frac{1}{4}$) turn   180°($\frac{1}{2}$) turn

Smaller shapes can rotate around the outside of larger shapes or on the inside of larger shapes.

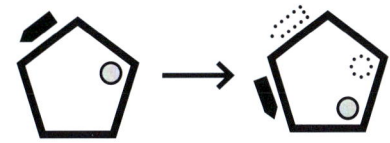

The Pencil Shape has moved Anticlockwise around the Pentagon and the Circle has moved Clockwise within the Pentagon.

Key Non-verbal Reasoning questions apply to rotations:

Example 1: Which shape completes the second pair of shapes?

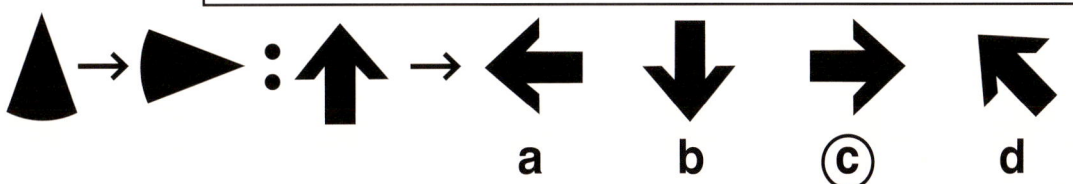

Answer: **c** - It has rotated 90° Clockwise (in the same way as the first pair).

Example 2: Which rotation is the odd one out?

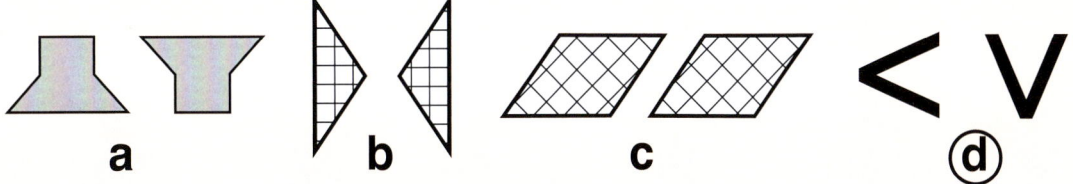

Answer: **d** - It has rotated 90° Anticlockwise but should rotate 180°.

Example 3: Which figure is next in the series?

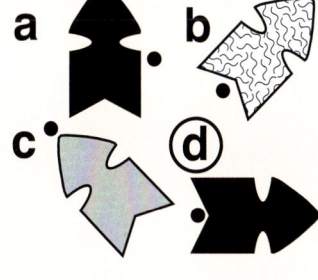

Answer: **d** - The Arrow rotates 45° Anticlockwise; the next Arrow must have a Black Fill; the Circle rotates 45° Clockwise around the centre (or 90° Clockwise around the Arrow).

Exercise 2: 2   Answer the following:

1) Which is the next figure in the series?

Answer _____   The Chevron Shape has been rotated clockwise _____°.
The Circle rotates within the Chevron in a(n) _____ direction.

2) Which pair of shapes does not rotate like the Test Shapes?

Answer _____   The shape has been rotated _____°.

3) Which shape rotates in the same way as the Test Shapes?

Answer _____   The shape has been rotated _____° _____.

4) Which figure is most like the Test Figure?

Answer _____   In comparison with the outer shape the inner shapes have rotated _____° and _____°.

5) Which line is the odd one out?

Answer _____   It spirals in a(n) _____ direction.

6) Which figure does not fit in with the other figures?

a   b   c   d   e

Answer ____   Why not? _____

7) Which shape belongs to this family of shapes?

a   b   c   d

Answer ____   Why? _____

8) Which pair of shapes does not rotate like the Test Shapes?

Test Shapes   a   b   c

Answer ____   This shape has been rotated _____°.

9) Which figure is next in the series?

a   b   c   d

Answer ____   The Kite rotates _____°.
The Heart rotates _____° around the Kite.

10) Which letter is missing from this family of letters?

S X H I N O

a D   b Z
c M   d F

Answer ____   Why? _____

Score

3. Superimposition

In Non-verbal Reasoning, shapes can be **Superimposed** onto other shapes. These superimpositions can include a **Merger**, an **Overlay**, a **Linkage** or an **Enclosure**.

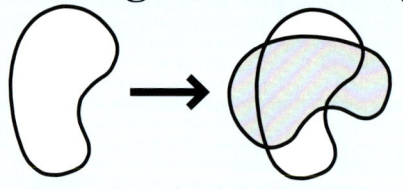 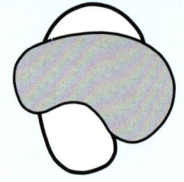 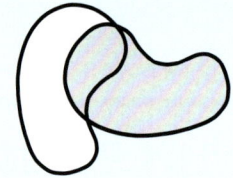 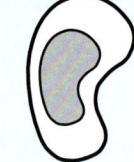

1. Merger   **2. Overlay**   **3. Linkage**   **4. Enclosure**

| Superimpositions have been indicated with a Grey Fill to help with visual clarity and ease of understanding. | The second shape Merges (crosses over) the first shape. The integrity (lines) of both shapes is retained. In this case it is a 90° rotation and inversion of the original shape. | The second shape Overlays (is on top of) the first shape. The original shape can be fully or partially covered. In this case it is a 90° rotation of the original shape. | The second shape is Linked to (does not cross over) the first shape. The integrity (lines) of both shapes is kept. Several shapes can be Linked together. | The second shape is Enclosed within the first shape. In this case a copy of the first shape is reduced in size and Enclosed within the original shape. |

Key Non-verbal Reasoning questions use superimpositions:

Example 1: Which figure is most similar to the Test Figure?

Test Figure   a   b   c   ⓓ

Answer: **d** - This is a rotated superimposed merger of 90°.

Example 2: Which superimposition is the odd one out?

  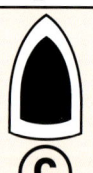  

a   b   ⓒ   d   e

Answer: **c** - The enclosed shape has not been rotated 180°.

Example 3: Which superimposition is next in the series?

Answer: **b** - The previous figure has been rotated 90°. The Cigar Shape with a Grey Fill overlays the Bone Shape.

Exercise 2: 3 Answer the following:

1) Which is the next figure in the series?

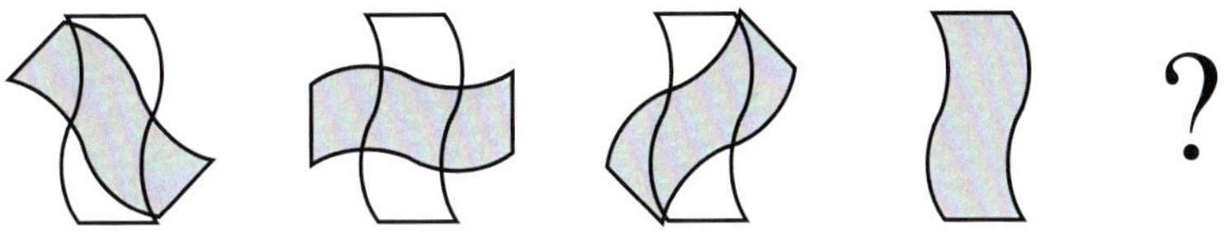

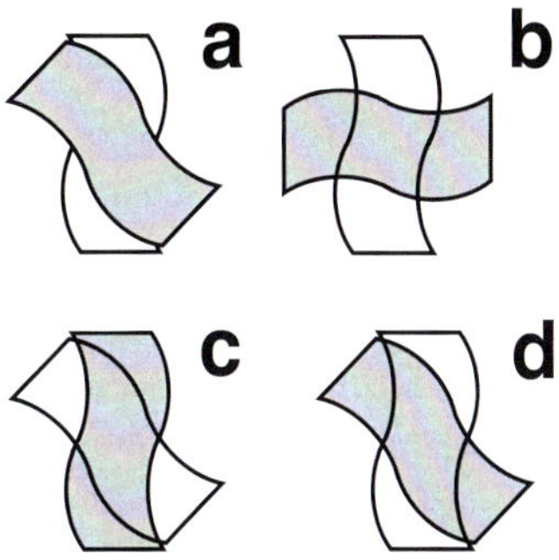

a b c d

Superimposition type: ____________________

Answer ____

2) Which figure does not fit in with the others?

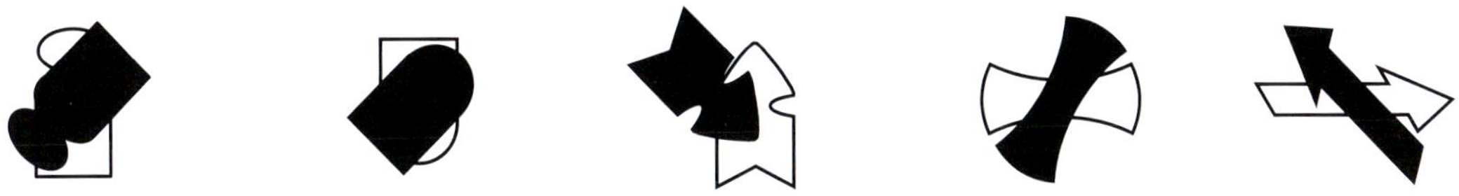

a b c d e

Answer ____ Superimposition type: ____________________

3) Which figure belongs to this family of figures?

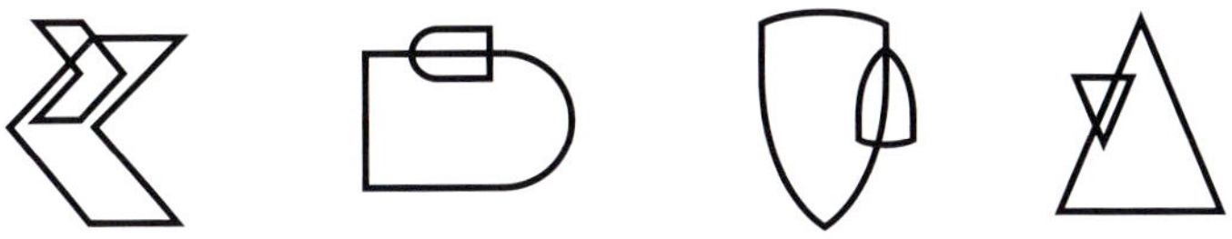

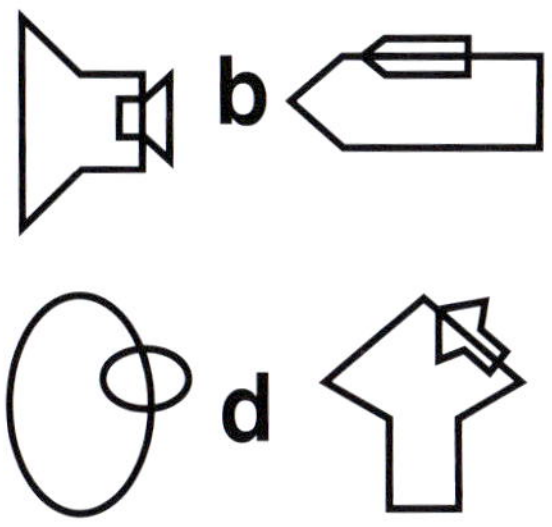

a b c d

Superimposition type: ____________________

Answer ____

4) Which figure is most like the Test Figure?

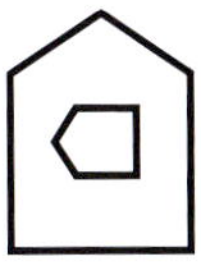

Test Figure

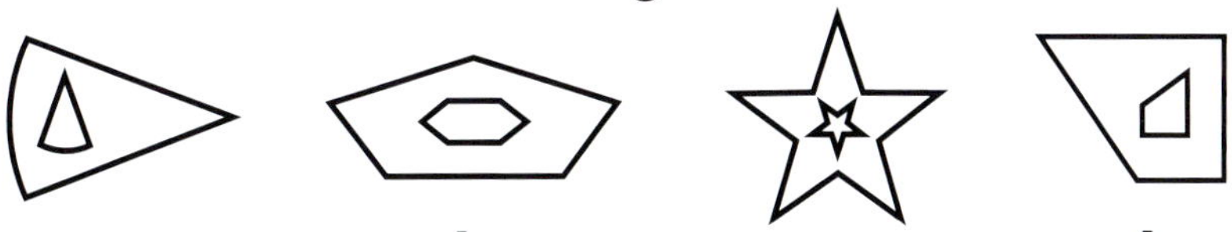

a b c d

Answer ____ Superimposition type: ____________________

5) Which figure is the odd one out?

a b c d e

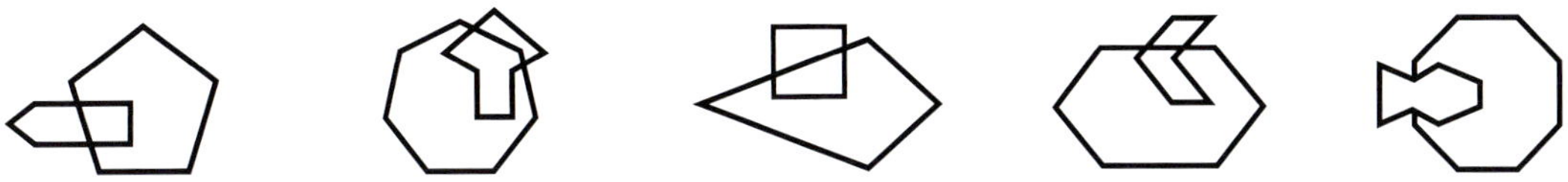

Answer ____ Superimposition type: ____________________

6) Which figure does not fit in with the others?

Answer ____
Superimposition types: _____ and _____

7) Which figure belongs to this family of figures?

Superimposition type:
Answer ____ _____

8) Which figure does not fit in with the other figures?

Answer ____ Superimposition type: _____

9) Which figure is next in the series?

Superimposition type:
Answer ____ _____

10) Which figure belongs to this family of figures?

Answer ____
Superimposition types:
_____ / _____ / _____

Score

28 © 2015 Stephen Curran

4. Transposition

In Non-verbal Reasoning, shapes can be **Transposed** or **Moved** from one position to another, either Horizontally or Vertically. Movements to the right or left are Horizontal, and movements up or down are Vertical. Some Transpositions involve both Vertical and Horizontal movements, i.e. a shape could move up and to the right.

Transpositions are enclosed to show movement.

1. Horizontal Transposition

2. Vertical Transposition

3. Horizontal and Vertical Transposition

Key Non-verbal Reasoning questions use transpositions:

Example 1: Which figure is most similar to the Test Figure?

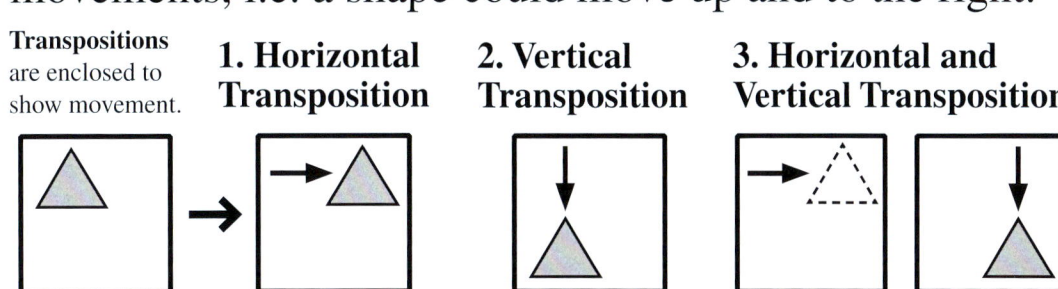

Test Figure   a   **b**   c

Answer: **b** - It is a Vertical and Horizontal transposition.

Example 2: Which transposition is the odd one out?

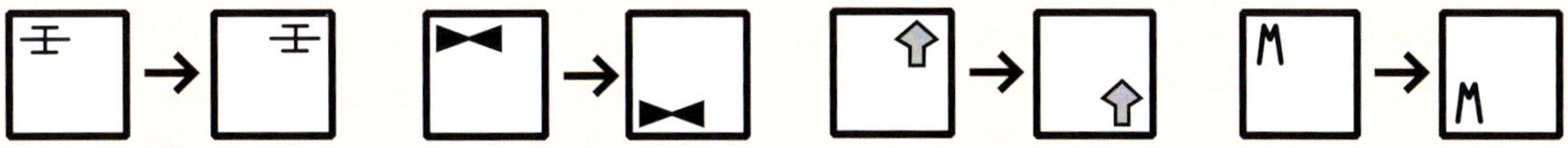

a   b   c   d

Answer: **a** - It is a Horizontal transposition.

Example 3: Which transposition is next in the series?

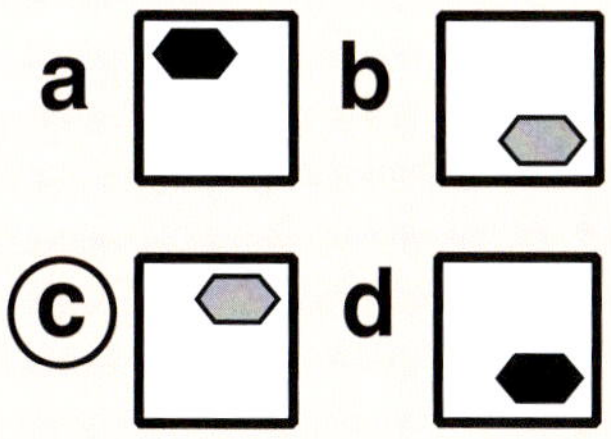

a   b   **c**   d

Answer: **c** - The Hexagon changes to a Grey Fill and transposes Vertically.

Exercise 2: 4   Answer the following:

1) Which figure is next in the series?

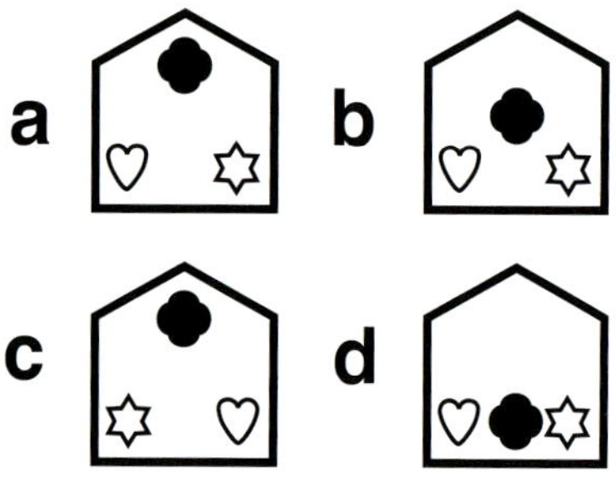

Answer ____   Transposition types:

Heart: __Horizontal__   Flower: _____   Star: _____

2) Which figure completes the second pair of figures?

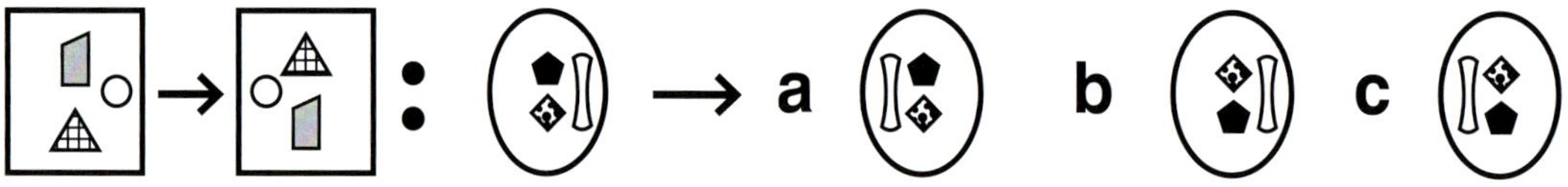

Transposition types: Pentagon: _____

Answer ____   Square: _____   Bone: _____

3) Which is the next figure in the series?

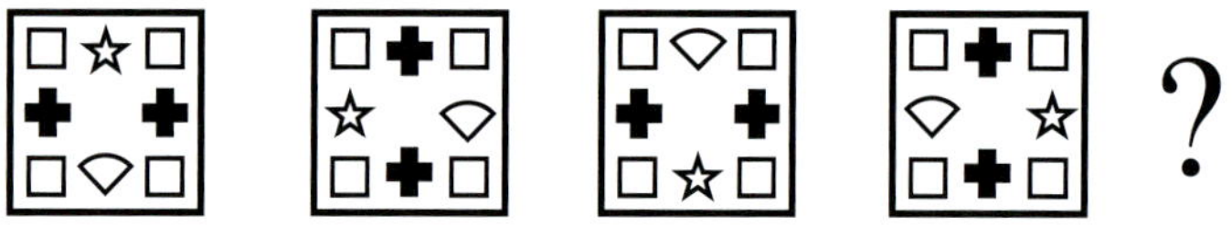

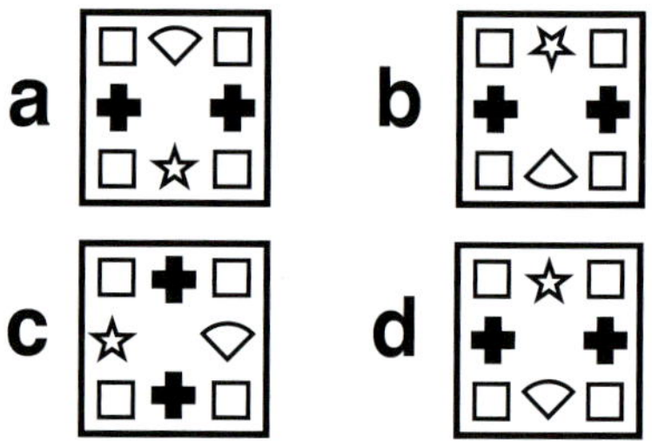

Answer: ____   Transposition types:

Star/Crosses/Sector: _____ and _____

4) Which pair of figures does not fit in with the others?

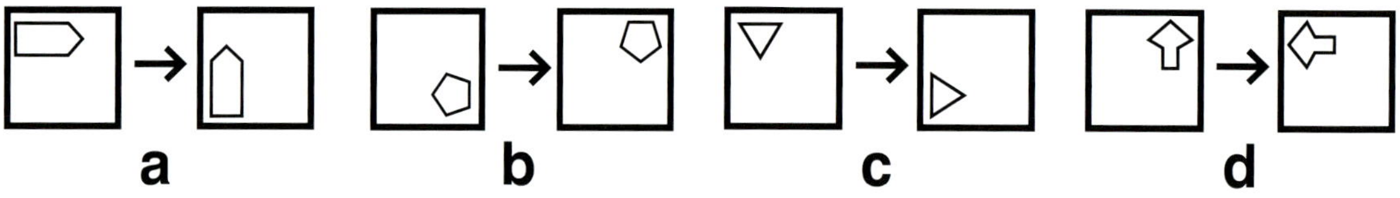

Transposition type:

Answer ____   _____

5) Which is the next figure in the series?

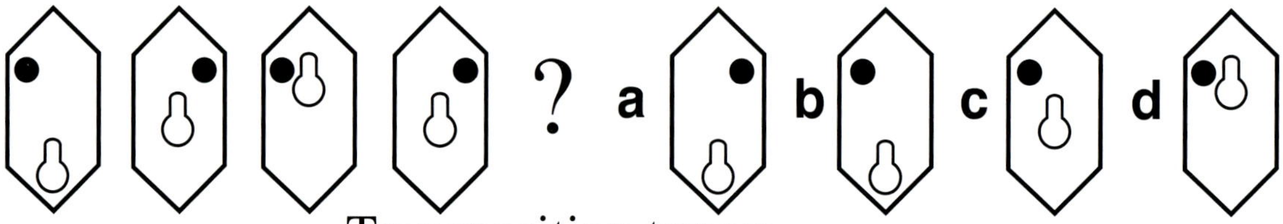

Transposition types:

Answer ____   Circle: _____   Keyhole: _____

6) Which figure completes the second pair of figures?

Answer ____   Transposition types:
Arrow: _____   Star: _____

7) Which pair of figures is the odd one out?

Answer ____   Transposition type: _____

8) Which pair of figures is most like the Test Figures?

Test Figures

Answer ____   Transposition types:
Square: _____   Pentagon: _____

9) Which figure is next in the series?

Answer ____
Transposition type: _____

10) Which pair of figures is most like the Test Figures?

Test Figures

Answer ____
Transposition types:
_____ and _____

Score ____

Chapter Three
MANIPULATIONS

In Non-verbal Reasoning, shapes can be **Manipulated** by:
Size • **Addition** • **Subtraction** • **Frequency**

1. Size

Shapes can **Increase** in size or **Decrease** in size:

1. **Enlargement** 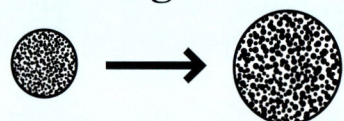 2. **Reduction**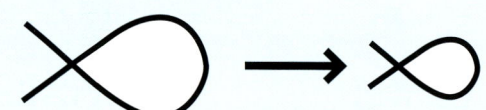

Key Non-verbal Reasoning questions apply to size change:

Example 1: Which shape completes the second pair of shapes?

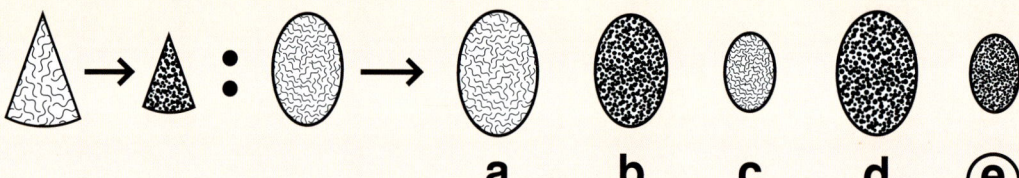

Answer: Shape **e** is a reduction and has a Speckled Fill.

Example 2: Which shape is different from the others?

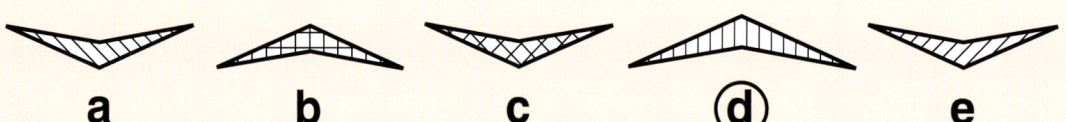

Answer: Shape **d** is an enlargement of the other shapes.

Example 3: Which shape is next in the series?

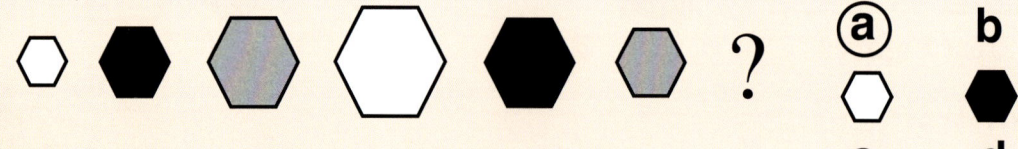

Answer: Shape **a** is a reduction (the next smallest) and has the correct fill.

Exercise 3: 1   Answer the following:

1) Which is the next figure in the series?

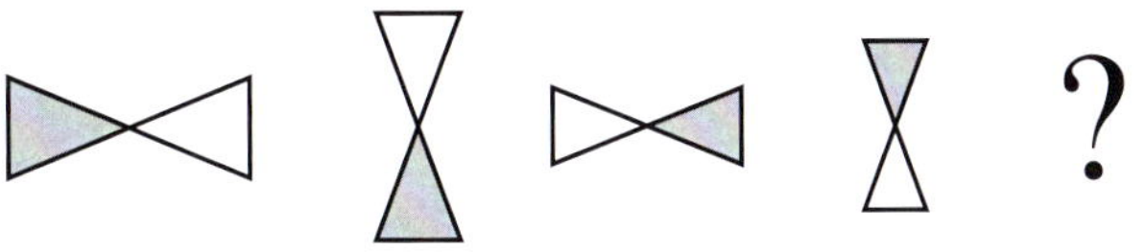

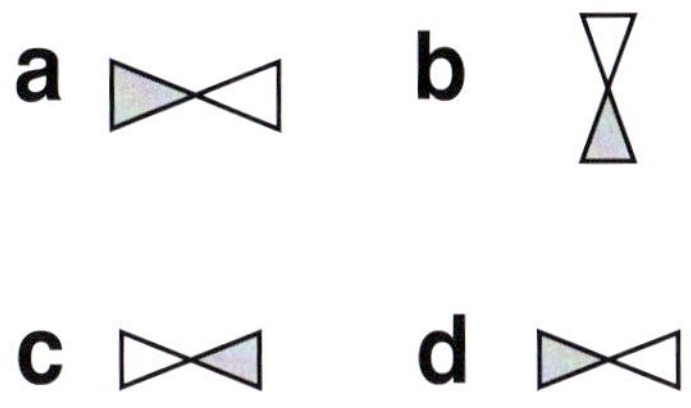

Answer ____

The change of size is a(n) _____Reduction_____.

2) Which shape does not fit in with the others?

Answer ____   The change of size is a(n) _____.

3) Which pair of figures is most similar to the Test Figures?

Test Figures

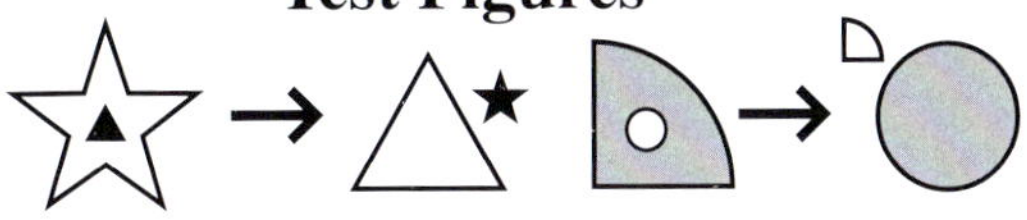

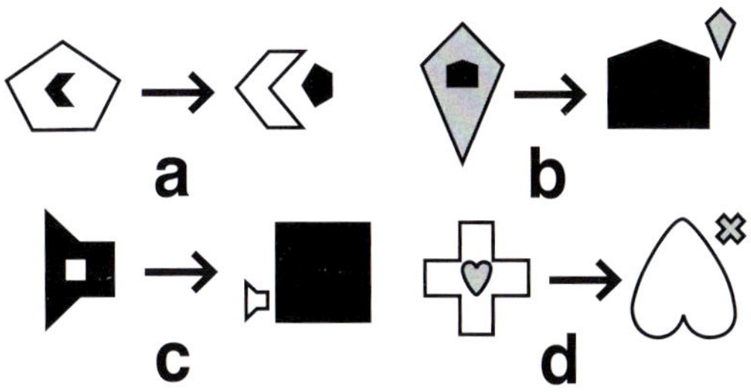

Answer ____   Name the shapes:

The _____ Shape reduces.
The _____ Shape enlarges.

4) Which pair of figures is most like the Test Figures?

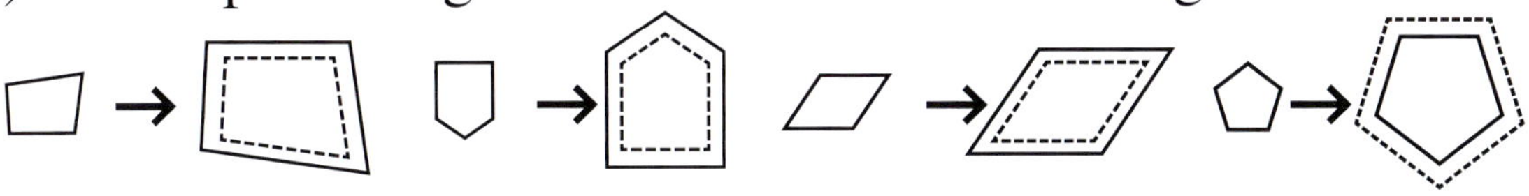

Test Figures

Answer ____   The change of size is a(n) _____.

5) Which is the next figure in the series?

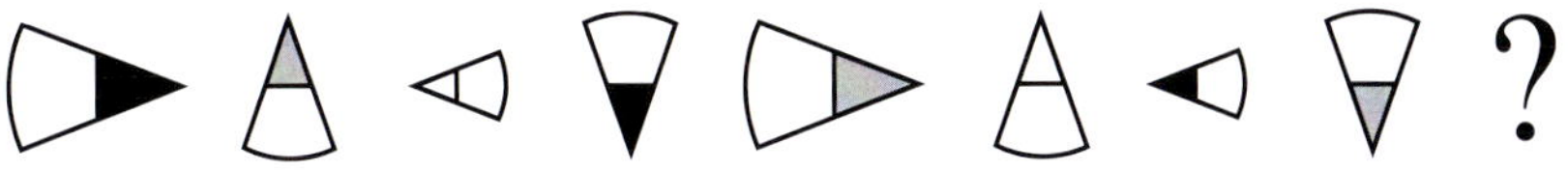

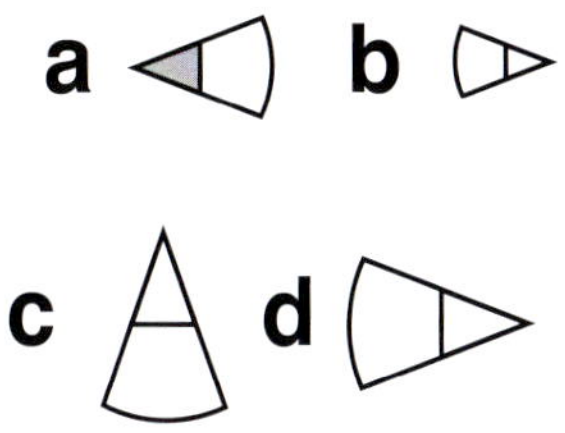

Answer ____   The change of size is a(n) _____.

© 2015 Stephen Curran

6) Which pair of figures does not fit in with the other figures?

a   b   c   d

Answer _____   The change of size is a(n) _____.

7) Which figure belongs to this family of figures?

Answer _____
The outer shape is a(n) _____ of the enclosed shapes.

8) Which figure does not fit in with the others?

a   b   c   d   e

Answer _____   The change of size starting at the centre is a(n) _____.

9) Which figure is the odd one out?

a   b   c

Answer _____   The change of size is a(n) _____.

10) Which figure belongs to this family of figures?

Answer _____
The enclosed shape is a(n) _____ of the outer shape.

Score

2. Addition

In Non-verbal Reasoning, one or more shapes can be **Added** to the original shape or separate additional shapes can be added.

1. Additions to shapes

The original shape has been copied, rotated 90° and superimposed onto the original shape. Additions are often combined with rotations, reflections, superimpositions and inversions.

2. Additional shapes

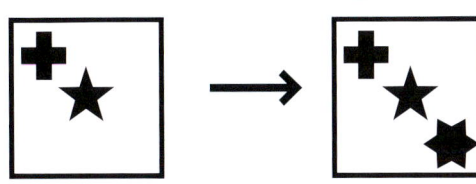

A third shape has been added to the two original shapes. This can also be understood as a change in Frequency (see pages 41-43).

Key Non-verbal Reasoning questions apply to additions:

Example 1: Which shape has an addition to the Test Shape?

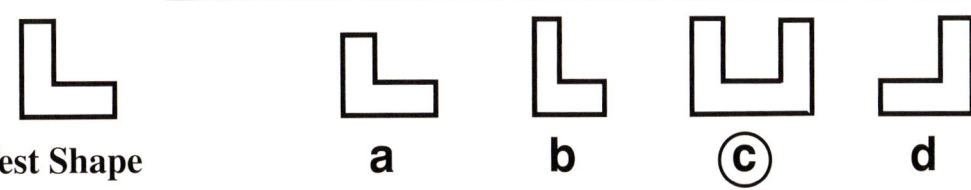

Answer: **c** - The original shape has received an addition.

Example 2: Which shape has no additions to the Test Shape?

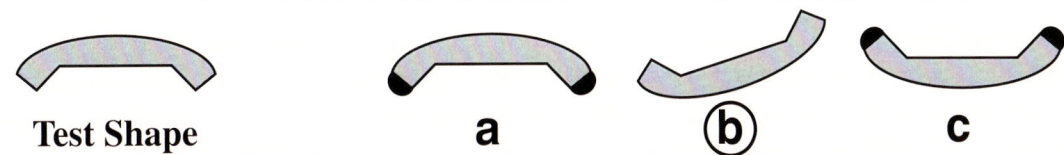

Answer: **b** - The shape has been rotated but has no additions.

Example 3: Which figure is next in the series?

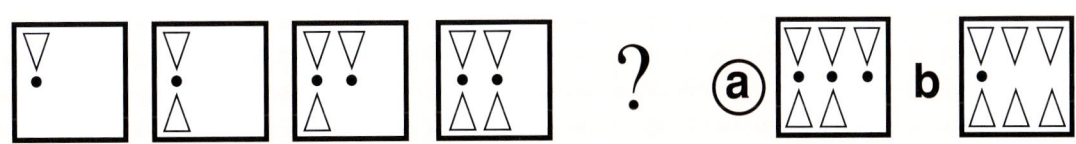

Answer: **a**

This has an addition of one Triangle with a White Fill at the top of the square and one more Circle with a Black Fill in the middle.

© 2015 Stephen Curran

Exercise 3: 2   Answer the following:

1) Which is the next figure in the series?

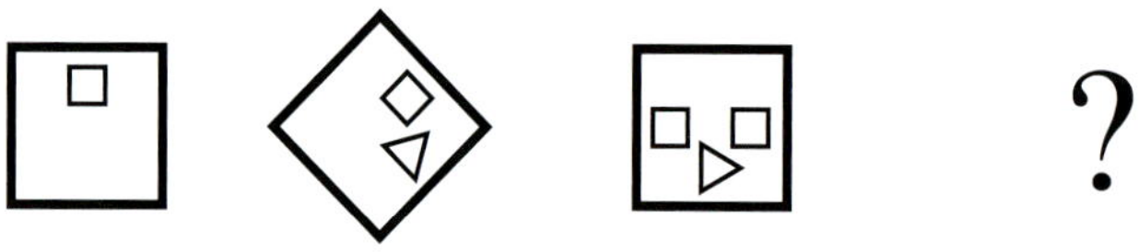

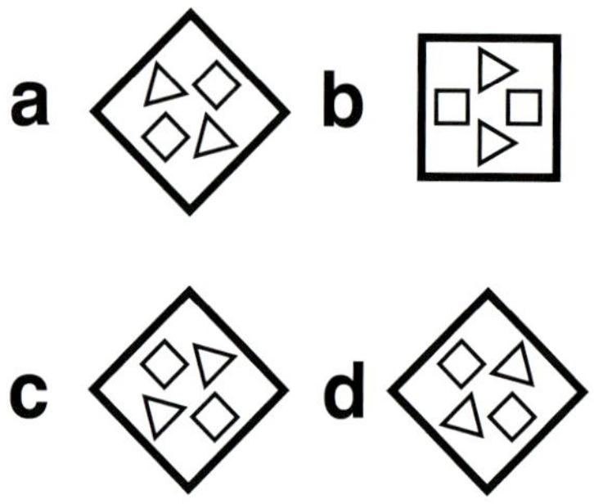

Name the shape that should be added:
Answer ____ _____

2) Which pair of figures does not fit in with the others?

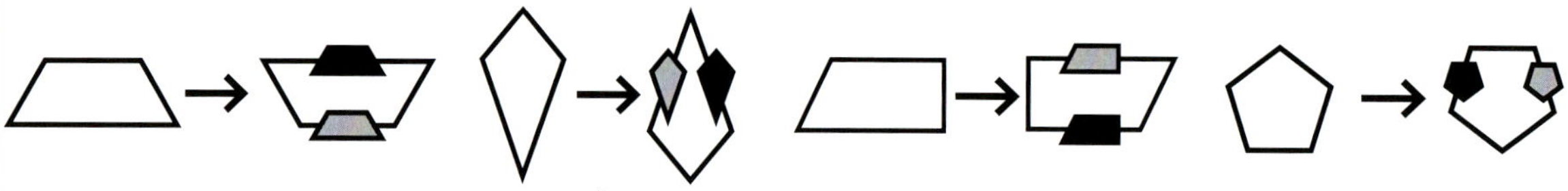

Answer ____   The incorrect shapes are _____ .

3) Which pair of figures belongs to this family of figures?

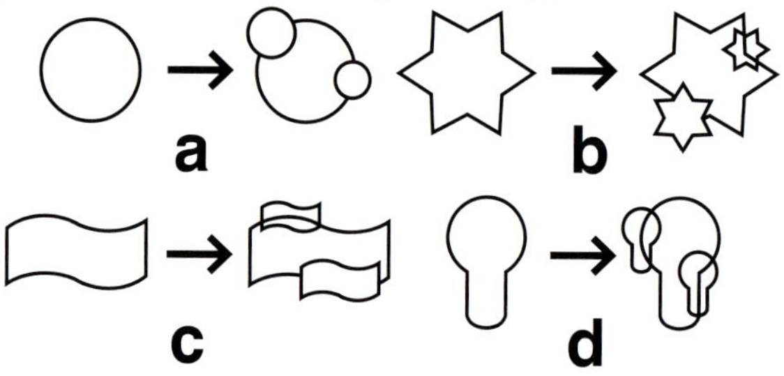

Answer ____
One linked and one overlayed
_____ shape must be added.

4) Which pair of figures is most like the Test Figures?

Test Figures

Answer ____   Three _____ shapes with _____ Fills must be added.

5) Which pair of figures is the odd one out?

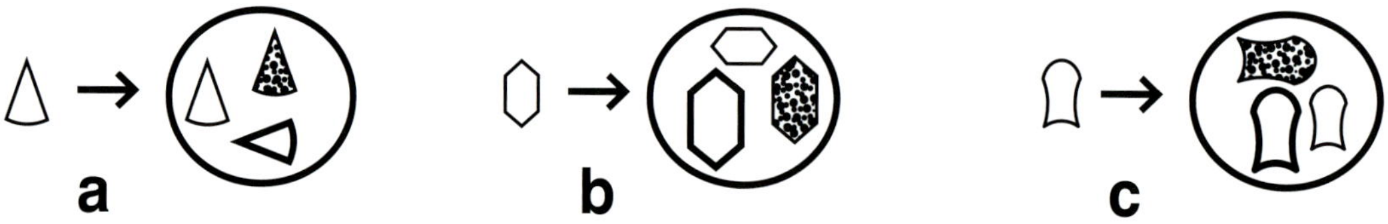

Answer ____   How many larger shapes should have been added? _____ shapes

6) Which pair of figures does not fit in with the other figures?

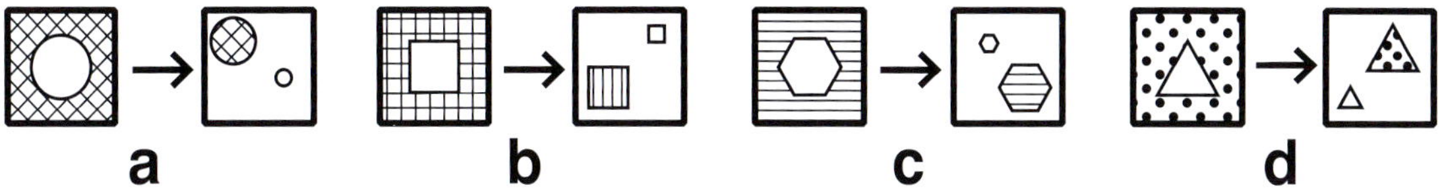

    a   b   c   d

Answer ____   The medium sized shape should have a _____ Fill.

7) Which pair of figures is most like the Test Figures?

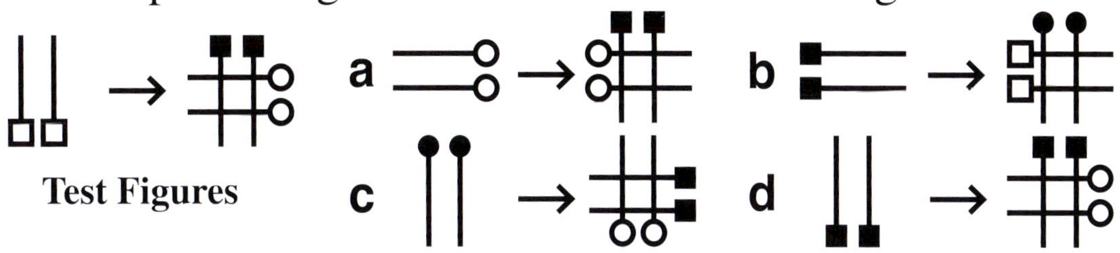

Test Figures

    a   b   c   d

Answer ____   How many shapes need to be added? _____ shape(s)

8) Which pair of figures does not fit in with the others?

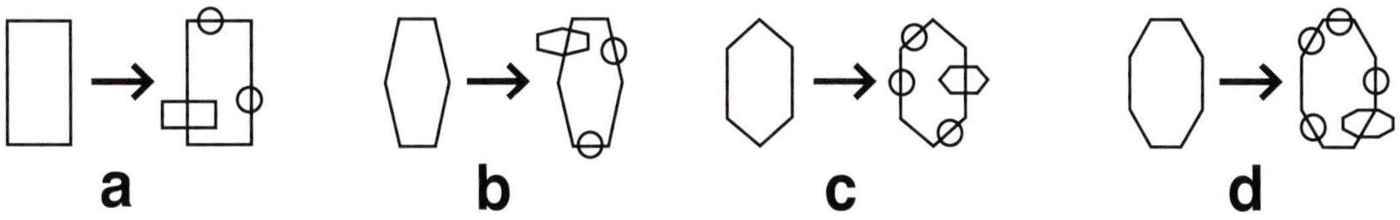

    a   b   c   d

Answer ____
Why not? _____

9) Which is the next figure in the series?

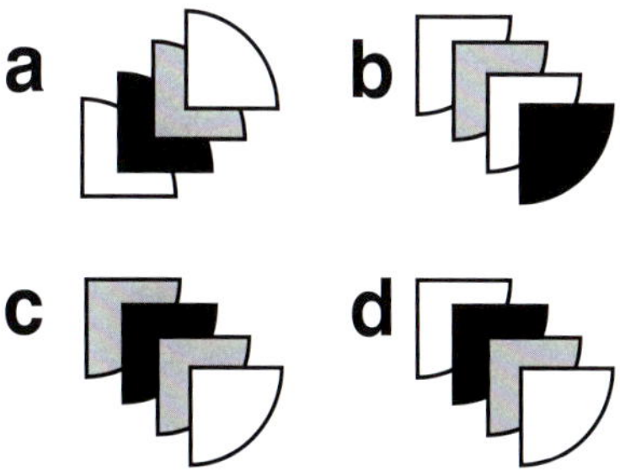

    a   b   c   d

Answer ____
The correct order of block fills is:
_____ _____ _____ _____

10) Which pair of figures belongs to this family of Figures?

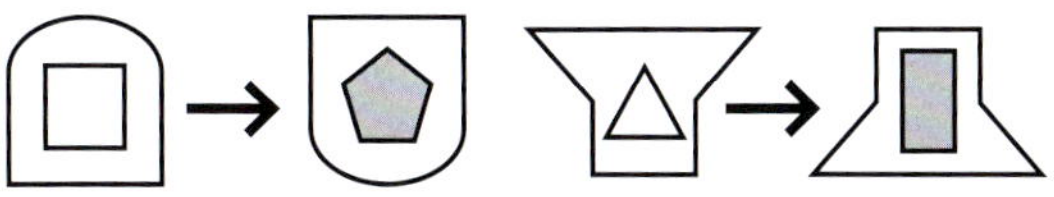

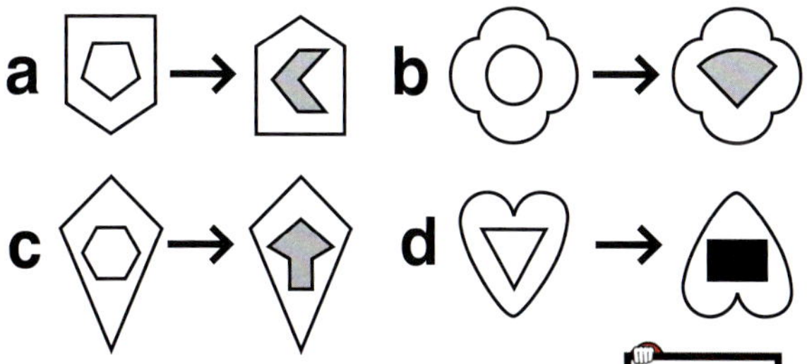

    a   b   c   d

Answer ____
The three rules are:
i) _____
ii) _____
iii) _____

Score

3. Subtraction

In Non-verbal Reasoning, smaller shapes or parts of a shape can be **Subtracted** from the original shape or shapes.

1. Subtracting parts of shapes

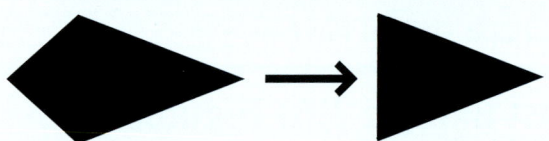

The original Kite with a Block Black Fill has had a Triangular section subtracted from it. The shape that remains is an Isosceles Triangle with a Block Black Fill.

2. Subtracting shapes

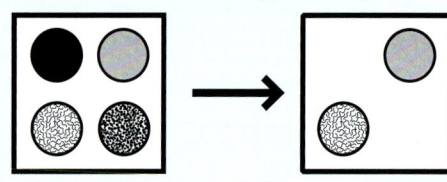

The Circles with a Speckled Fill and a Block Black Fill have been subtracted from the original group. This can also be understood as a change in Frequency (see pages 41-43).

Key Non-verbal Reasoning questions apply to subtractions:

Example 1: Which shape is a subtraction of the Test Shape?

 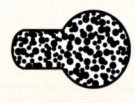   

Test Shape   a   b   ⓒ   d

Answer: **c** - It has a subtraction or missing piece.

Example 2: Which shape is not a subtraction of the Test Shape?

Test Shape   a   b   c   ⓓ

Answer: **d** - This shape has been rotated but it is the same.

Example 3: Which figure is next in the series?

    ?   ⓐ    b

   c    d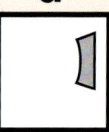

Answer: **a**

It is a 90° Anticlockwise rotation. The Ribbon Shape with a Block Black Fill is subtracted as it moves to the bottom left of the square.

Exercise 3: 3   Answer the following:

1) Which is the next figure in the series?

Answer ____

A(n) _____ of the Octagon must be subtracted each time in a(n) _____ direction around the shape.

2) Which pair of figures does not fit in with the others?

Answer ____   What two things must be subtracted each time?
i) _____   ii) _____

3) Which figure is next in the series?

What two things must be subtracted?
Answer ____   i) _____   ii) _____

4) Which pair of figures does not fit in with the others?

Why not? _____
Answer ____   _____

5) Which is the next figure in the series?

Answer ____
What is the order of subtraction? (Underline the correct answer.)
Clockwise or Anticlockwise.

6) Which two pairs of shapes are most alike?

a   b   c   d

Answer ____ and ____ Which two things must be subtracted each time?
i) _____ ii) _____

7) Which pair of figures is the odd one out?

a   b   c   d

Answer ____ What must be subtracted each time?
_____

8) Which pair of figures is most like the Test Figures?

Test Figures   a   b   c

Which two things must be subtracted?
Answer ____ i) _____ ii) _____

9) Which figure is next in the series?

a   b   c   d

Answer ____

What must be subtracted? _____

10) Which pair of figures is most like the Test Figures?

Test Figures   a   b   c

Answer ____ Which two things must be subtracted?
i) _____
ii) _____

Score

4. Frequency (Counting)

In Non-verbal Reasoning, **Frequency** involves the counting of shapes, smaller shapes within other shapes, or parts of shapes.

1. Counting shapes

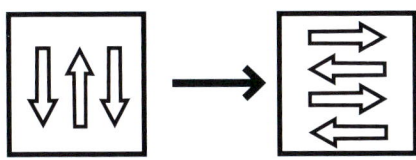

The original figure has three Vertical Arrows. The frequency (number) in the second figure is increased to four Horizontal Arrows. **This change could also be understood as an addition.**

2. Counting parts of shapes

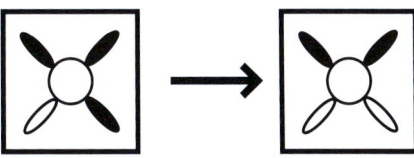

The original figure has three Ellipses with a Black Fill. The frequency (number) in the second figure is decreased to two Ellipses with a Black Fill. **This change could also be understood as a subtraction.**

Key Non-verbal Reasoning questions apply to frequency:

Example 1: Which figure is most similar to the Test Figure?

   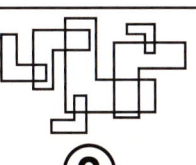 

Test Figure   **a**   **b**   **ⓒ**   **d**

Answer: **c** - It has a frequency of six like the Test Figure.

Example 2: Which figure is most different from the others?

    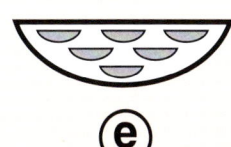

a   **b**   **c**   **d**   **ⓔ**

Answer: **e** - It has a frequency of six rather than seven.

Example 3: Which figure is next in the series?

 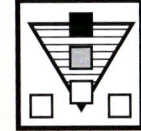    

a   **ⓑ**

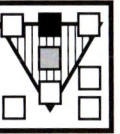  

c   **d**

Answer: **b**

The frequency (number) of Squares should be eight. The fill types of the Squares are not relevant. The Equilateral Triangle should point upwards and have Vertical Shading.

Exercise 3: 4   Answer the following:

1) Which is the next figure in the series?

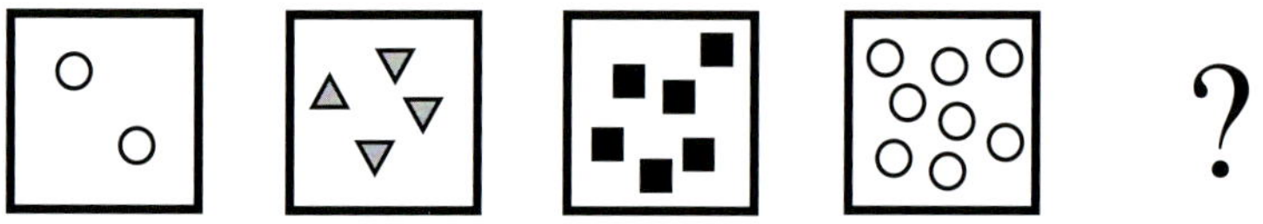

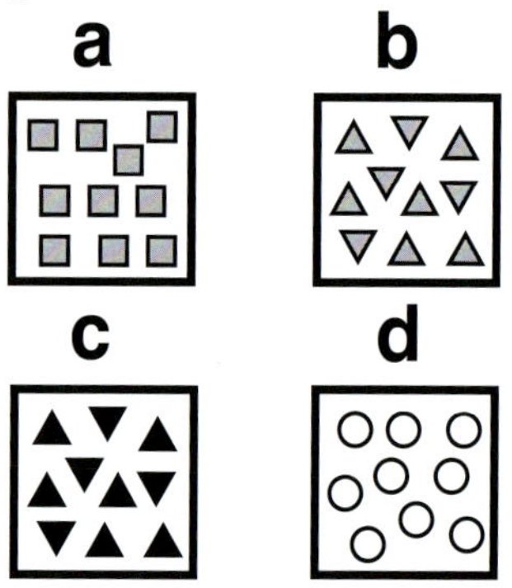

Answer ____
Write out the number sequence of the five figures.
It begins with **2**, _____

2) Which figure does not fit in with the others?

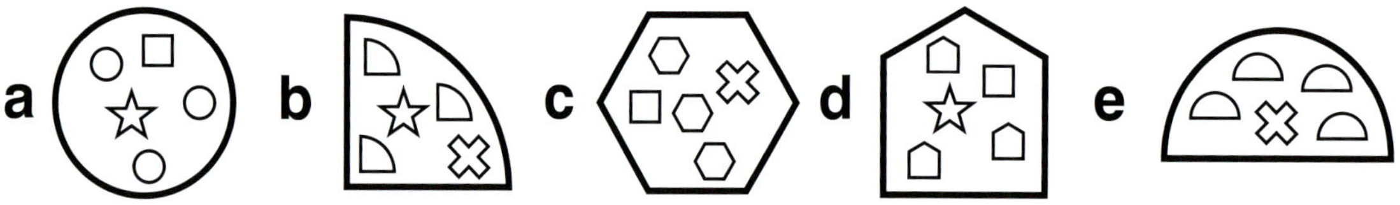

Answer ____   Why not? _____

3) Which figure belongs to this family of figures?

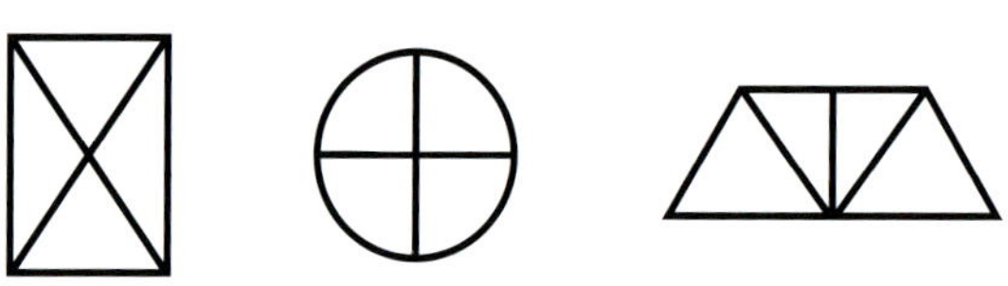

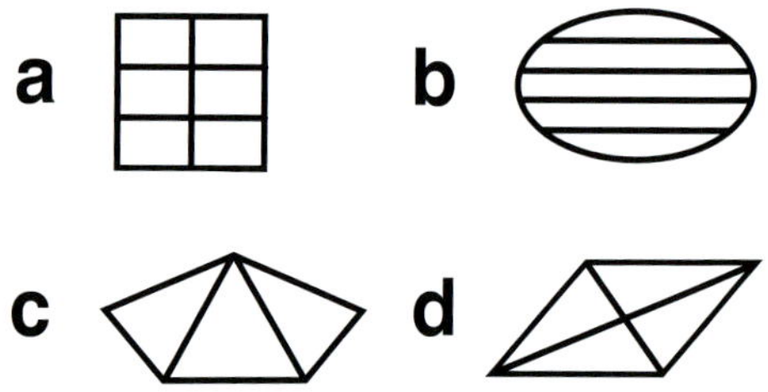

Answer ____   The shapes should be divided into ____ parts.

4) Which pair of figures is most like the Test Figures?

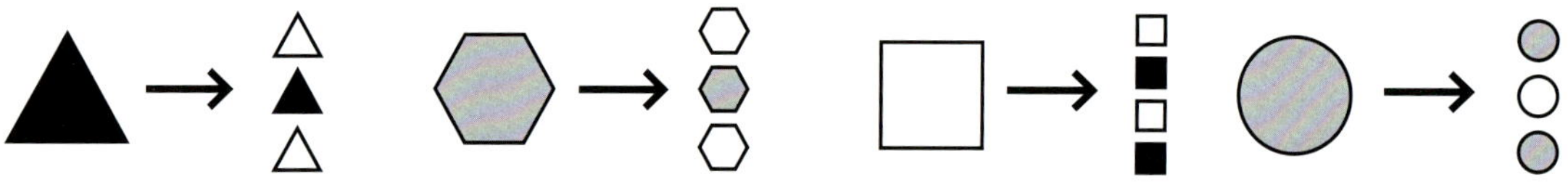

Test Figures

Answer ____   How many smaller shapes should there be? ____

5) Which pair of figures is the odd one out?

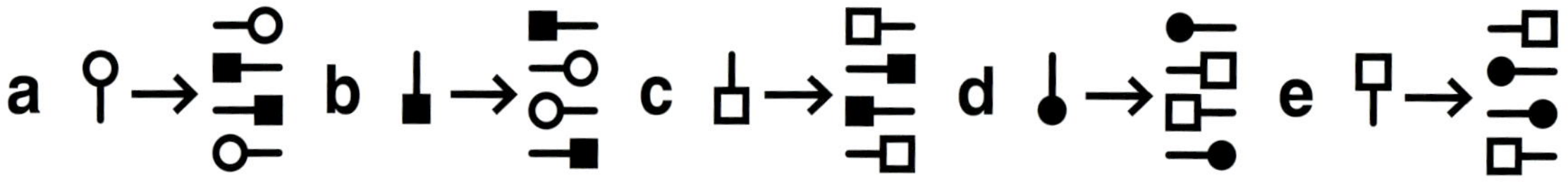

Answer ____   Why? _____

6) Which figure does not fit in with the other figures?

Why not? _____

Answer ____ _____

7) Which figure belongs to this family of figures?

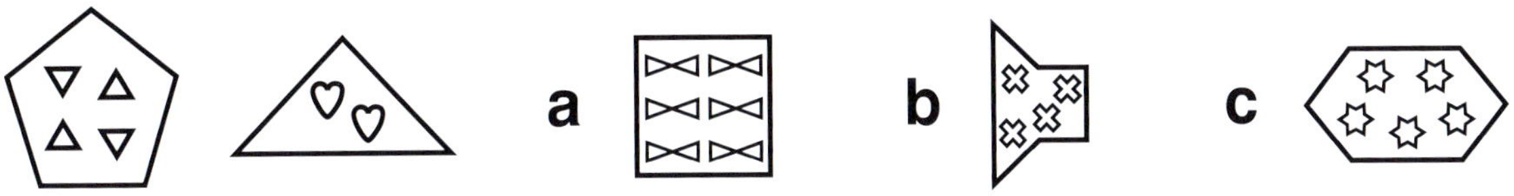

Answer ____   There should be ____ enclosed shape(s).

8) Which figure does not fit in with the others?

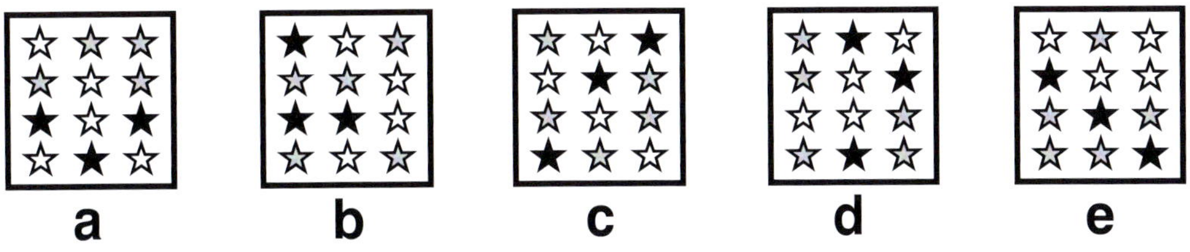

Answer ____   There should be ___ Black Stars and ___ Grey Stars.

9) Which is the next figure in the series?

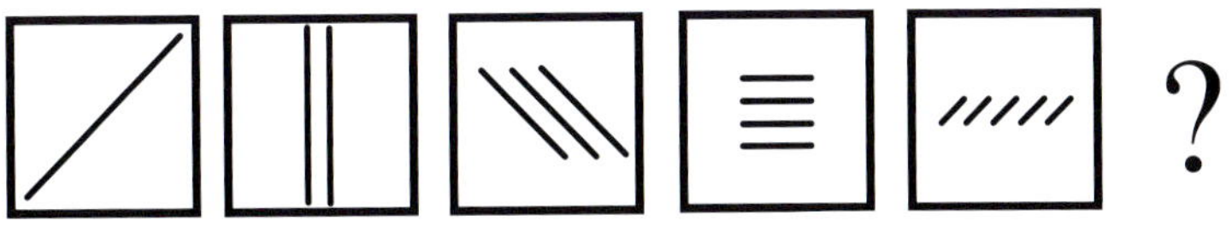

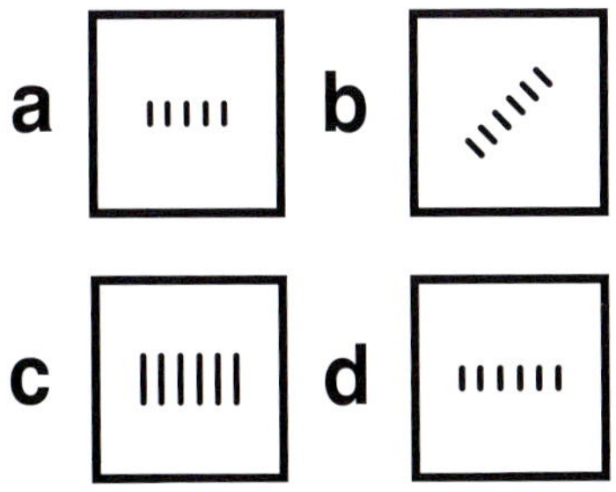

Answer ____
Write out the number sequence of the six figures.
It begins with **1**, _____

10) Which figure belongs to this family of figures?

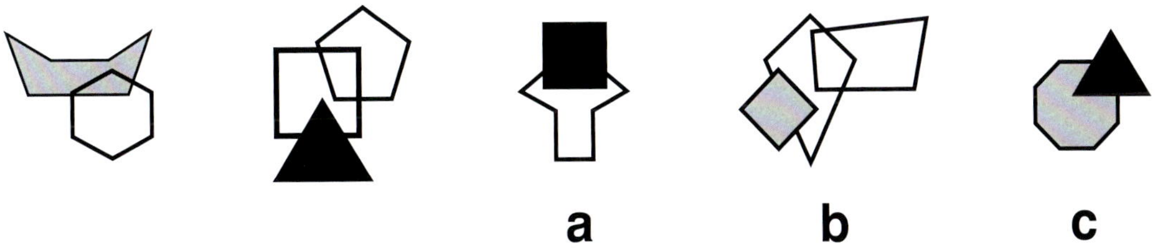

Answer ____   Why? _____
_____

Score

Chapter Four
PATTERNS

In Non-verbal Reasoning, shapes can make **Patterns** in two ways:
Repetition • Cumulation

1. Repetition

Shapes can be be arranged in a **Repetitive** pattern:

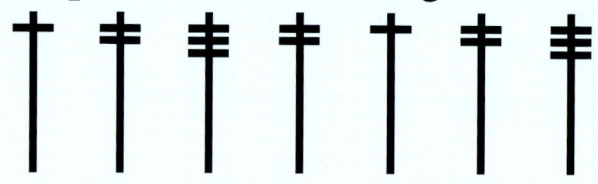

The Telegraph Poles are in a repetitive pattern of one, two, three, two, one, two, three crossbars, etc.

Key Non-verbal Reasoning questions apply to repetition:

Example 1: Which shape is first in the series?

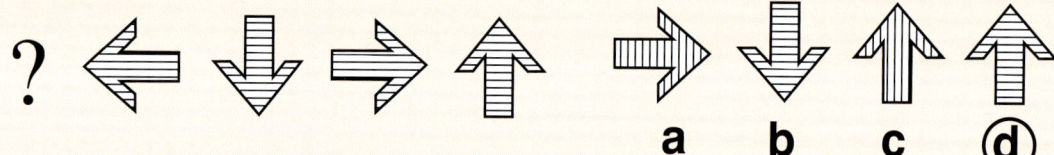

Answer: **d** - It has the correct shading and rotation.

Example 2: Which shape is missing in the series?

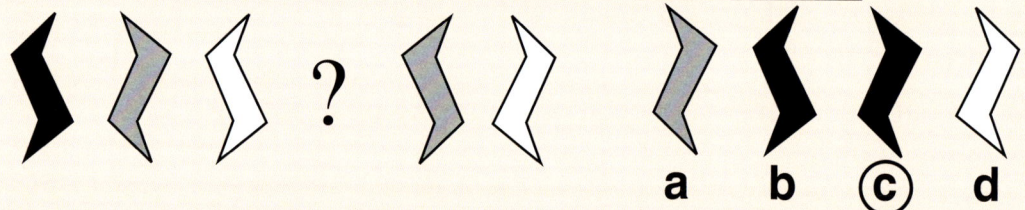

Answer: **c** - It has a Black Fill and is the correct reflection.

Example 3: Which figure is next in the series?

Answer: **c** - Both shapes have the correct fill and rotation.

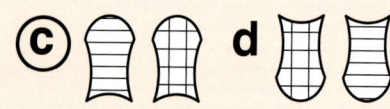

Exercise 4: 1   Answer the following:

1) Which is the next figure in the series?

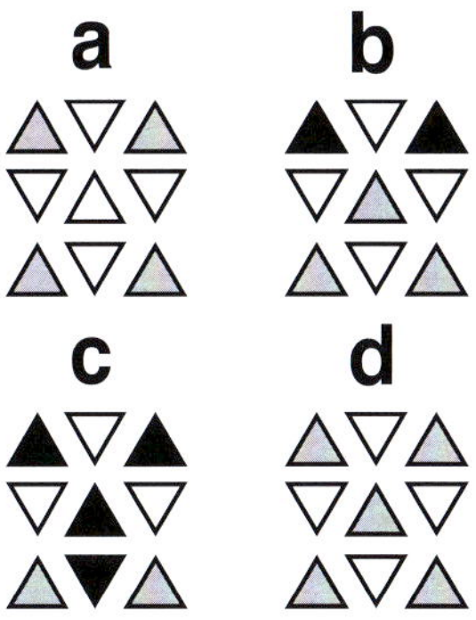

Answer ____
Write out the repetitive pattern of the Triangles with a Grey Fill in numerical terms: _____

2) Which figure is first in the series?

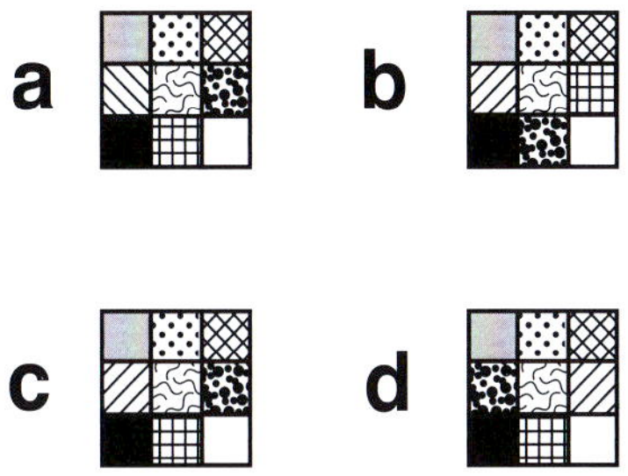

Answer ____ Do the fills rotate Clockwise or Anticlockwise? _____

3) Which is the missing figure in the series?

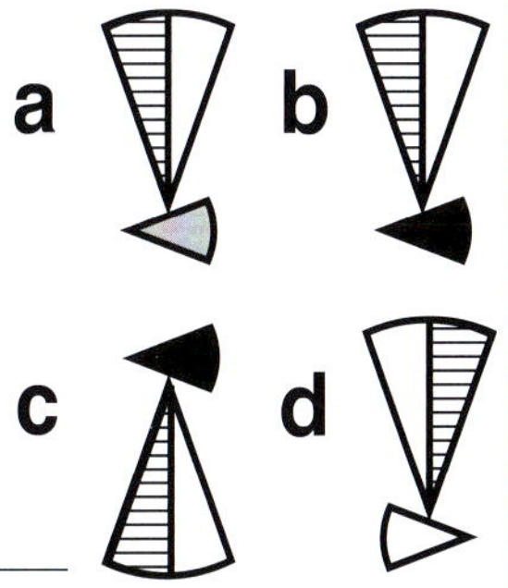

Answer ____ After the figure has been inverted, the large Sector undergoes which movement? _____

4) Which is the next figure in the series?

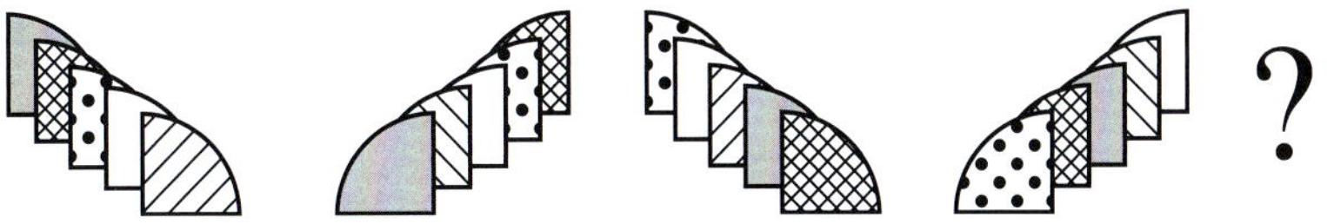

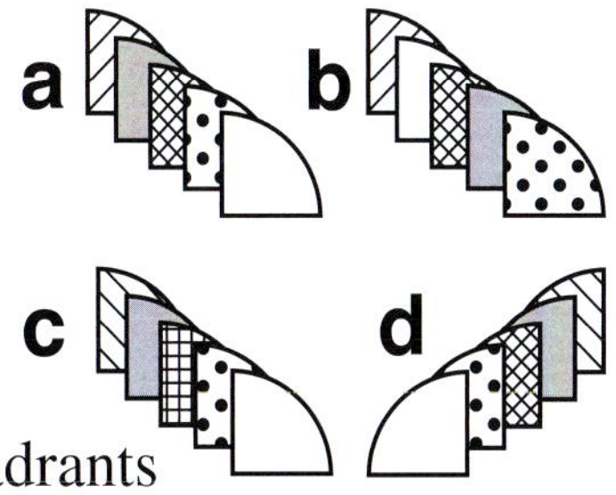

Answer ____
Write out the order of fills (front to back) for the Quadrants given in the answer: _____

5) Which figure is first in the series?

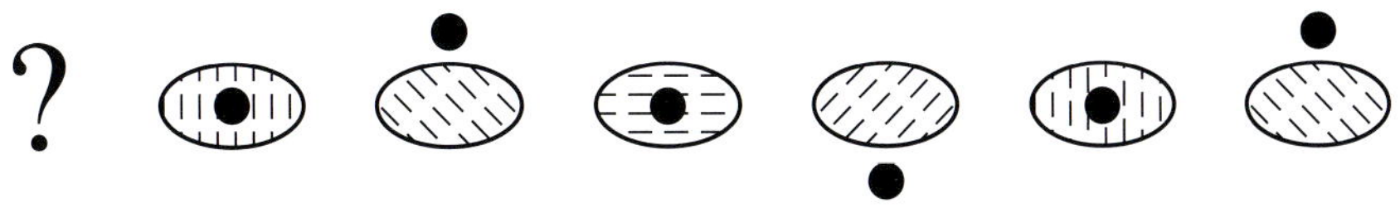

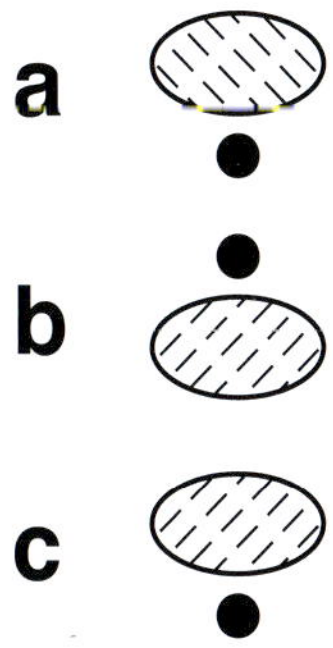

Answer ____
Describe the fill of the Ellipse in this figure.
_____

6) Which is the missing figure in the series?

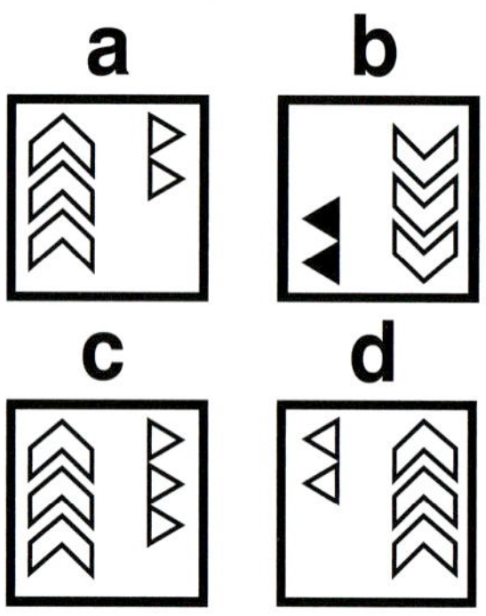

Answer ____ Write out the repetitive pattern of the Triangles in numerical terms: _____

7) Which figure is next in the series?

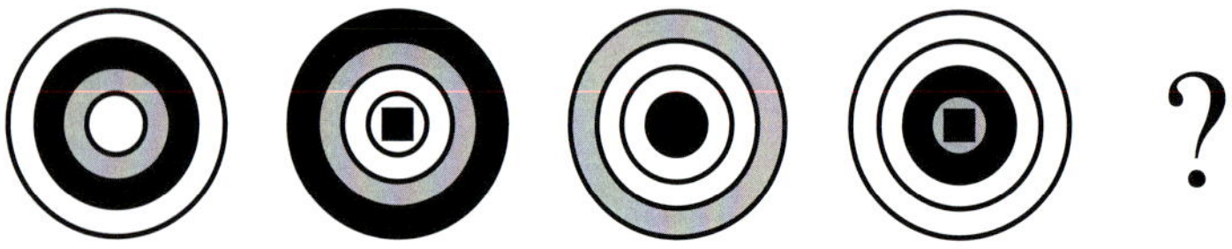

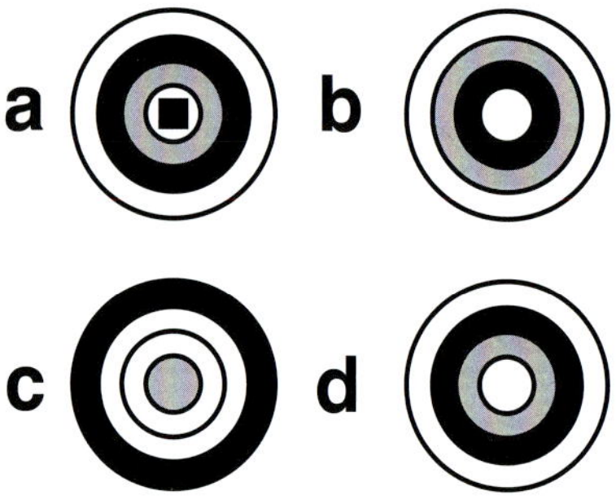

Answer ____ Which shape is repeated in every other figure of the series? _____

8) Which figure is next in the series?

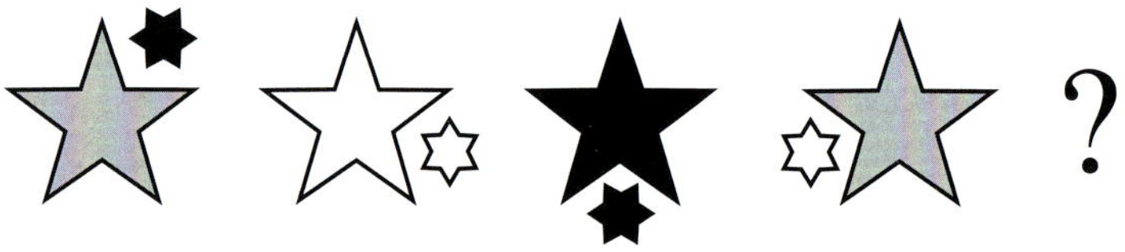

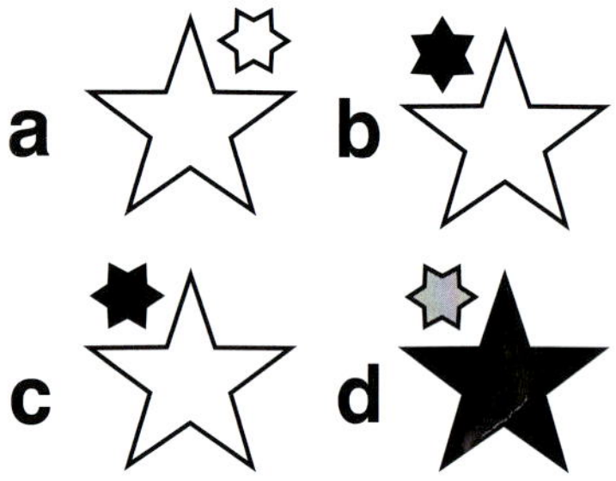

Answer ____ Write out the order of fills for the Five-pointed Star: _____

9) Which figure is missing in the series?

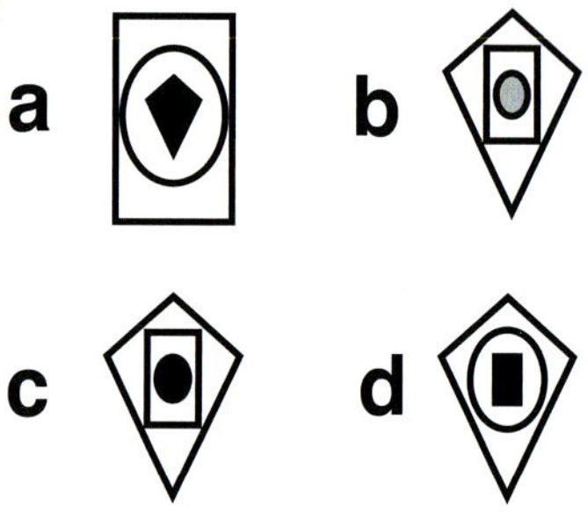

Answer ____ Describe the three-fold size progression for the Rectangle: _____ _____ _____

10) Which is the next figure in the series?

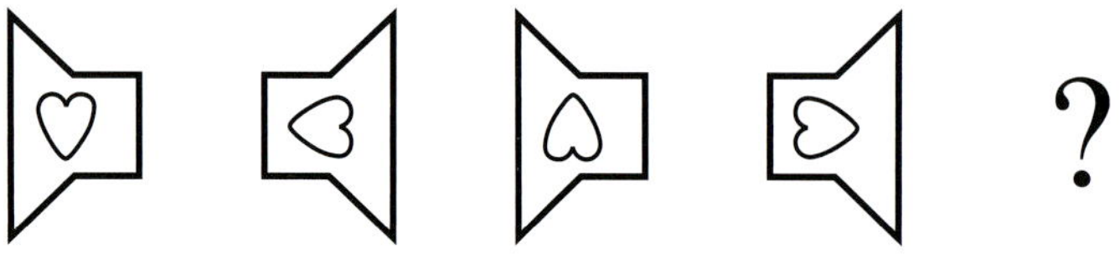

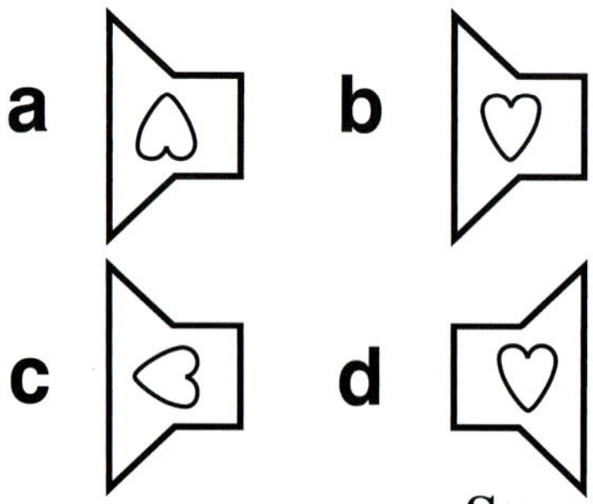

Answer ____

The Heart rotates in a(n) _____ direction.
The Speaker reflects along the _____ axis.

Score

2. Cumulation

Shapes can be be arranged in a **Cumulative** pattern:

    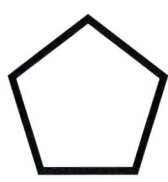

The Pentagon builds side by side in five stages.

Key Non-verbal Reasoning questions apply to cumulation:

Example 1: Which shape is first in the series?

 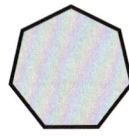      a   b

c  d

Answer: **b** is a larger shape and has the correct Liquid Fill.

Example 2: Which figure is missing in the series?

 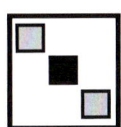 ?  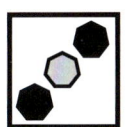   a 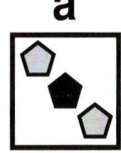 b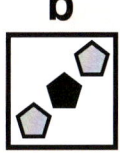

c 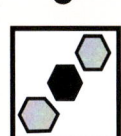 d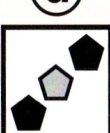

Answer: **d** has Pentagons that lie diagonally from bottom left to top right and has a fill order of Black, Grey, Black.

Example 3: Which figure is next in the series?

   ? a  b 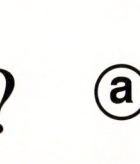 c  d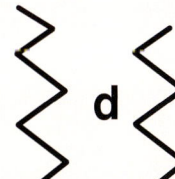

Answer: **a** has six lines so it is the correct Zigzag Line Shape. It is also the correct direction of the Zigzag Line Shape.

Exercise 4: 2   Answer the following:

1) Which is the next figure in the series?

Answer ____   Why? _____
_____

2) Which figure is first in the series?

Answer ____   Name the two types of line used:
i) _____ _____ _____   ii) _____ _____ _____

3) Which is the missing figure in the series?

Answer ____   What shape must be added each time? _____

4) Which is the next figure in the series?

Answer ____   Which shape is cumulative? _____

5) Which figure is first in the series?

Answer ____   What two things must be added each time? _____ and _____

6) Which is the missing figure in the series?

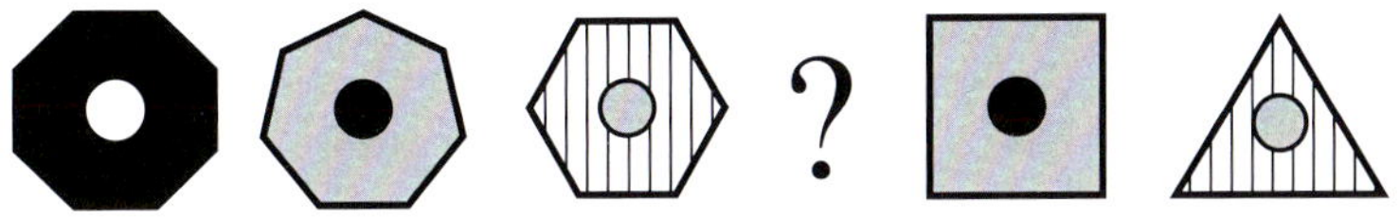

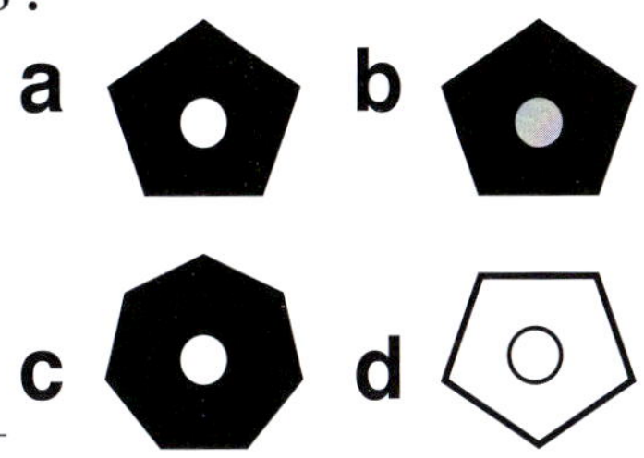

Answer _____ Why? _____
_____

7) Which is the next figure in the series?

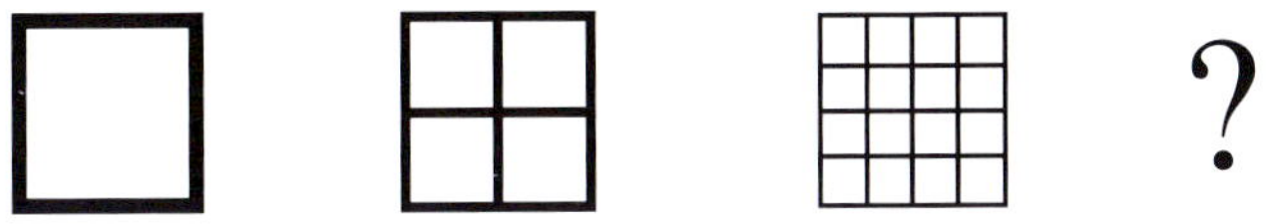

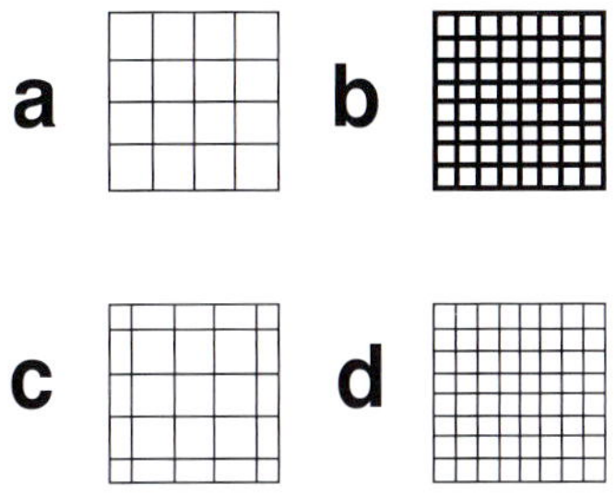

Answer _____ Name the two cumulative actions:
i) _____
ii) _____

8) Which figure is first in the series?

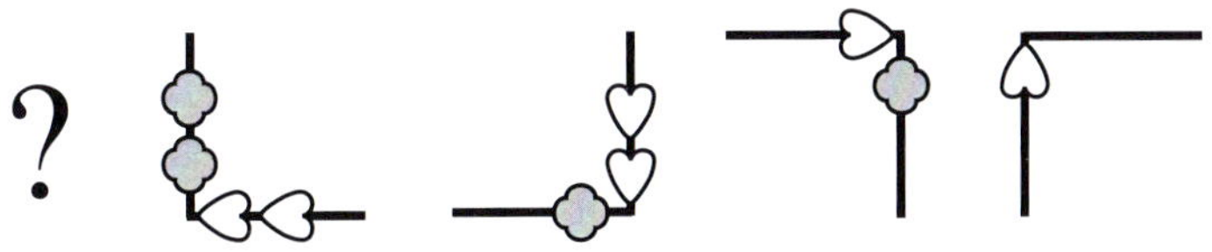

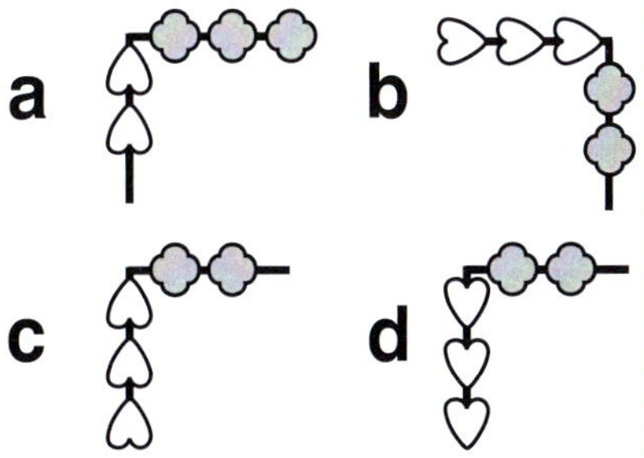

What must be subtracted?
Answer _____ _____

9) Which is the missing figure in the series?

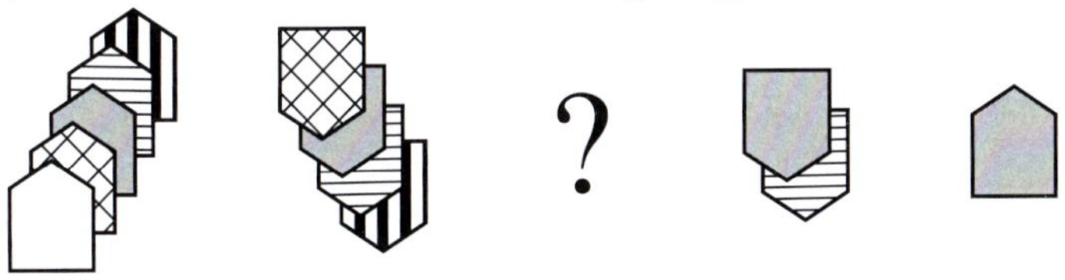

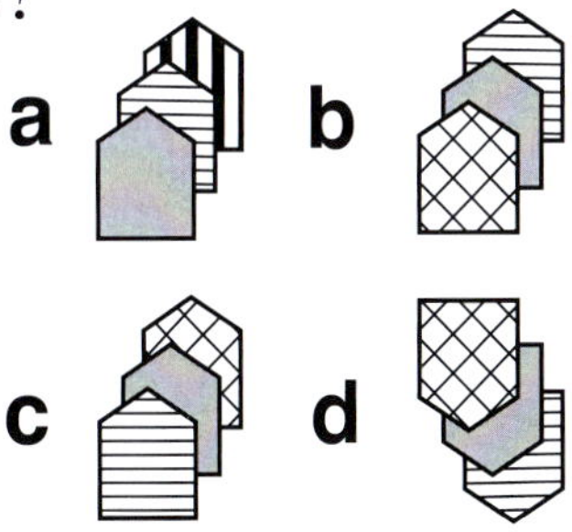

Answer _____ Which shape is subtracted?
_____

10) Which is the next figure in the series?

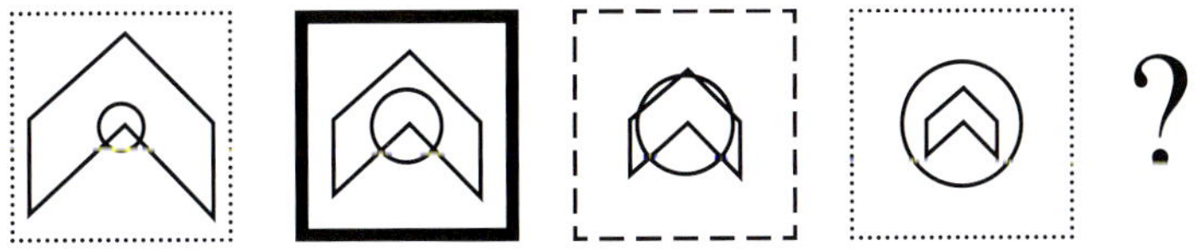

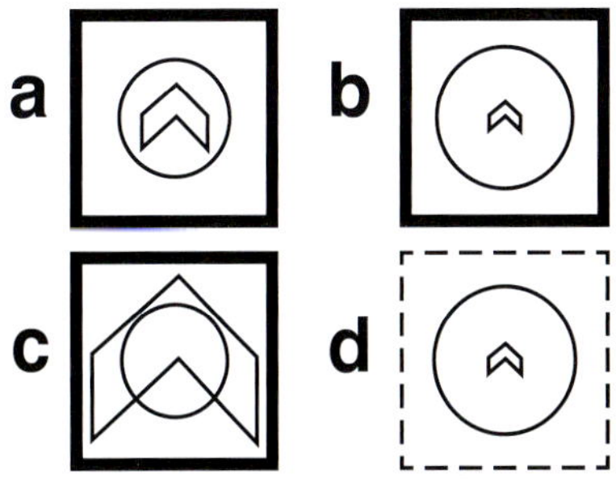

Answer _____
Write the repetitive pattern of the lines sequence
of the Squares: _____
What are the cumulative actions? _____

Score

Chapter Five
LAYERING

Non-verbal Reasoning questions are complicated by the process of **Layering**. Questions can have up to five layers (or changes) that have to be observed to find a solution.

1. Level One

Some shapes only have one layer or change.

Test Shape

The Segment Shape has received only one layer or change. It has been rotated 180°.

Key Non-verbal Reasoning questions apply to layering:

Example 1: Which shape is most similar to the Test Shape?

Test Shape   a   b   c   ⓓ

Answer: **d** is circular, as is the Test Shape.

Example 2: Which shape is most unlike the Test Shape?

Test Shape   a   b   ⓒ   d

Answer: **c** has a Black Fill; the Test Shape has a Speckled Fill.

Example 3: Which shape is next in the series?

a   ⓑ

c   d

Answer: **b** has been rotated 45° in an Anticlockwise direction.

Exercise 5: 1   Answer the following:

1) Which is the next shape in the series?

Answer ____

2) Which shape does not fit in with the others?

Answer ____

3) Which figure belongs to this family of figures?

Answer ____

4) Which figure is most like the Test Figure?

Test Figure

Answer ____

5) Which shape is the odd one out?

Answer ____

6) Which figure does not fit in with the others?

a b c d e

Answer ____

7) Which figure is most similar to the Test Figures?

Test Figures   a b c d

Answer ____

8) Which figure is the odd one out?

a b c d e

Answer ____

9) Which figure is next in the series?

? a b c d

Answer ____

10) Which figure is most similar to the Test Figures?

Test Figures   a b c

Answer ____

Score

2. Level Two

In Non-verbal Reasoning, questions can have two layers:

Test Shape   **Layer 1**   **Layer 2**

The Pencil Shape has two layers (undergoes two changes):
Layer 1 - It has been reflected or rotated 180°.
Layer 2 - The Block Black Fill becomes a Block Grey Fill.

Example 1: Which shape completes the second pair of shapes?

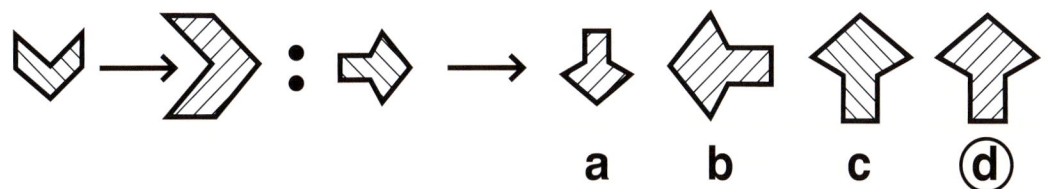

Answer: **d** - The shape enlarges and rotates 90° Anticlockwise (in the same way as the first pair).

Example 2: Which pair of shapes is the odd one out?

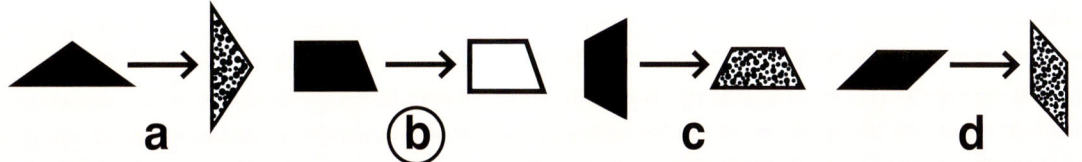

Answer: **b** does not rotate and has the wrong fill.

Example 3: Which figure is next in the series?

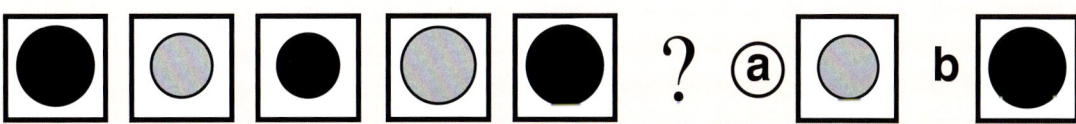

Answer: **a** has a Grey Fill (fills alternate) and it has a small Circle. (Pattern is two small Circles, then two large Circles, etc.)

Exercise 5: 2   Answer the following:

1) Which is the next figure in the series?

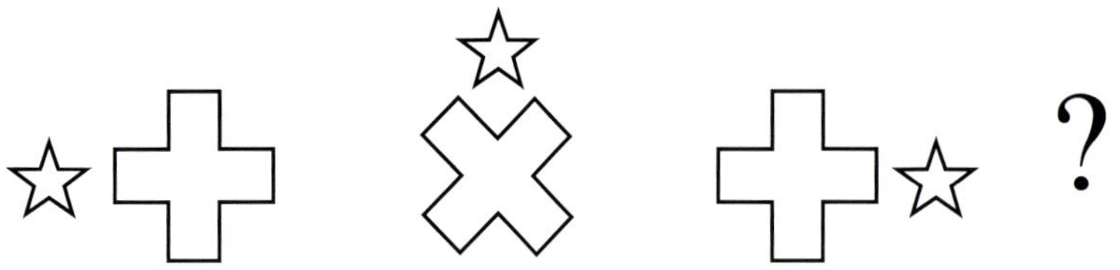

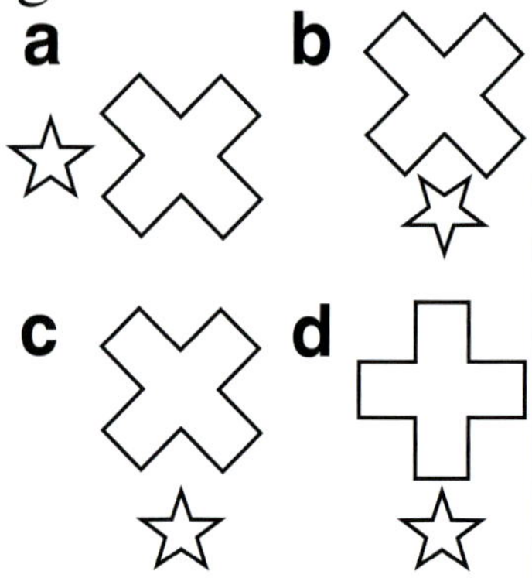

Answer ____

2) Which figure is most like the Test Figure?

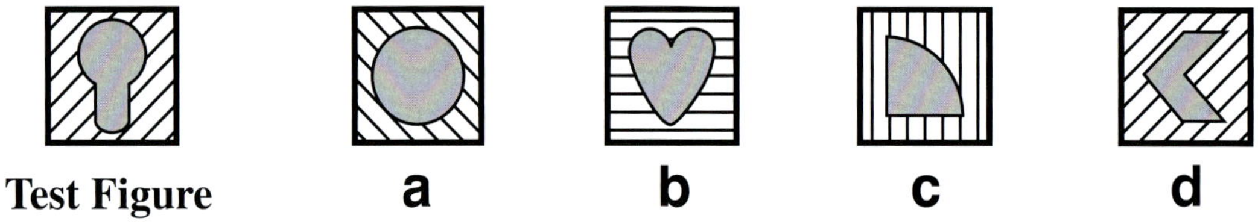

Test Figure

Answer ____

3) Which is the next figure in the series?

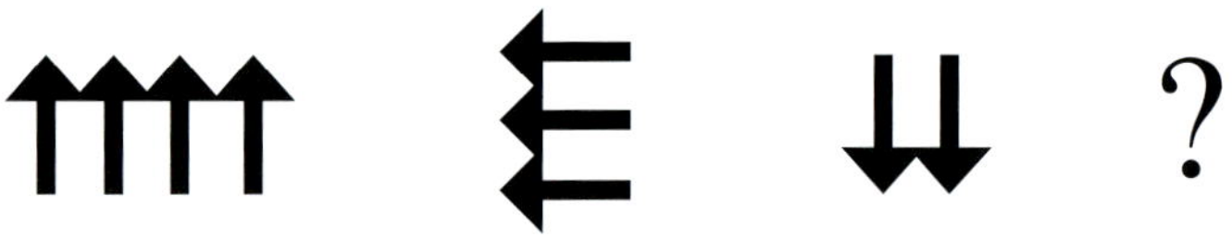

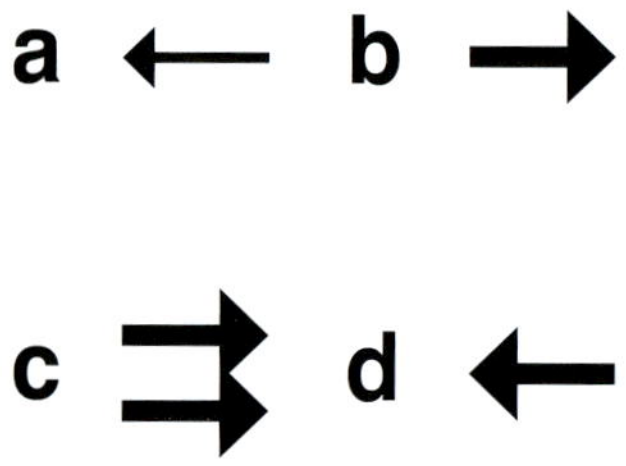

Answer ____

4) Which figure is most similar to the Test Figure?

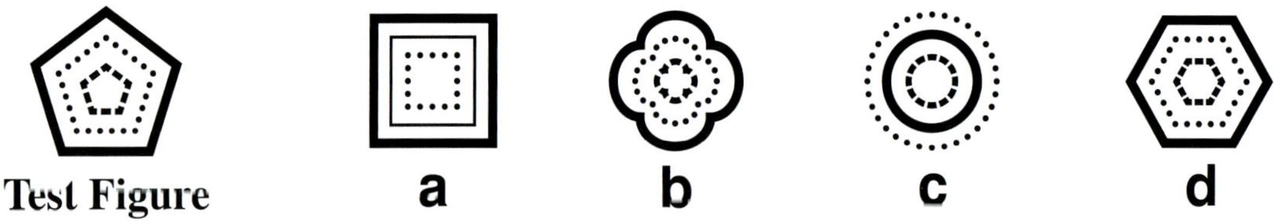

Test Figure

Answer ____

5) Which figure is next in the series?

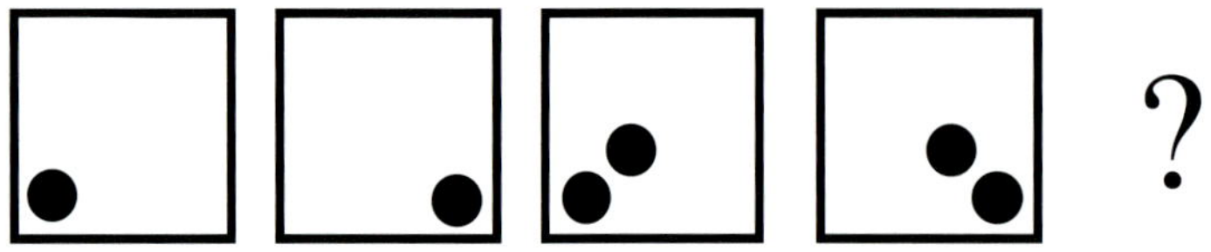

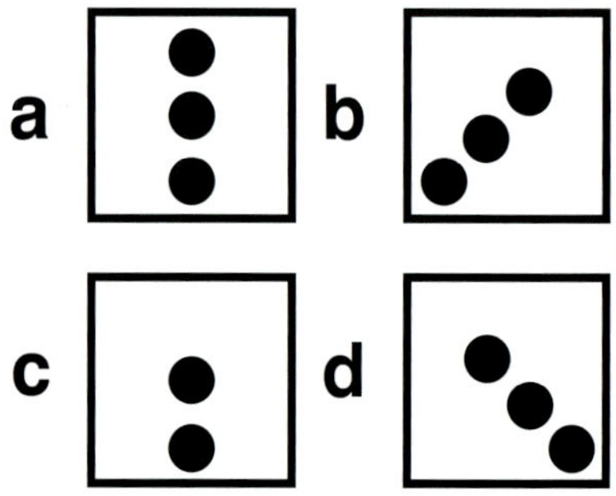

Answer ____

6) Which two figures are most similar?

a b c d e

Answer ____ and ____

7) Which figure is most like the Test Figure?

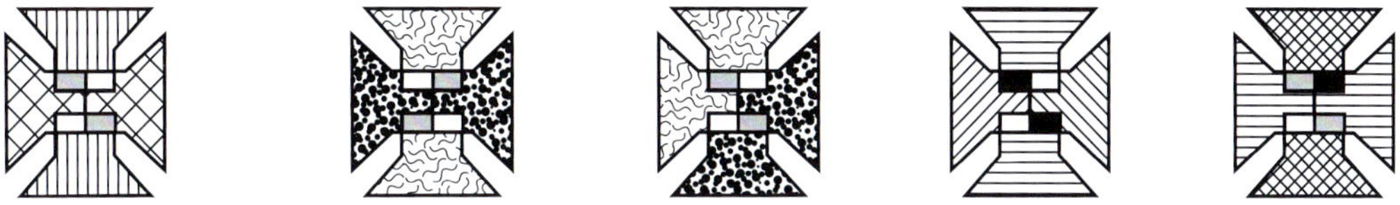

Test Figure   a   b   c   d

Answer ____

8) Which figure is most similar to the Test Figure?

Test Figure   a   b   c   d

Answer ____

9) Which is the next figure in the series?

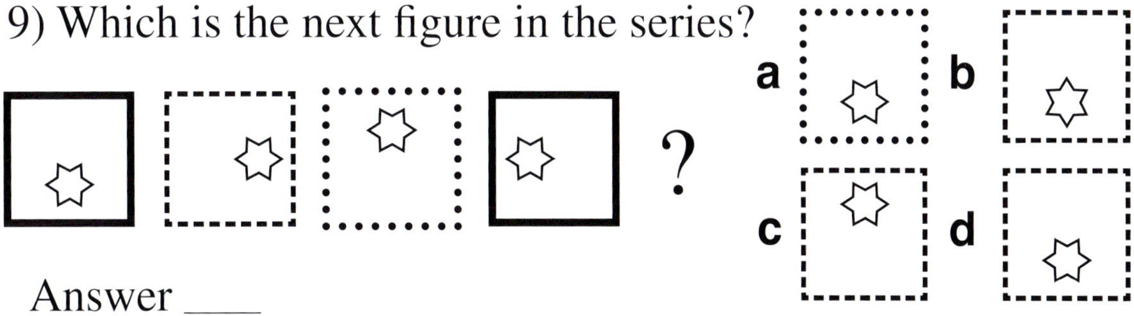

a b c d

Answer ____

10) Which figure is most like the Test Figure?

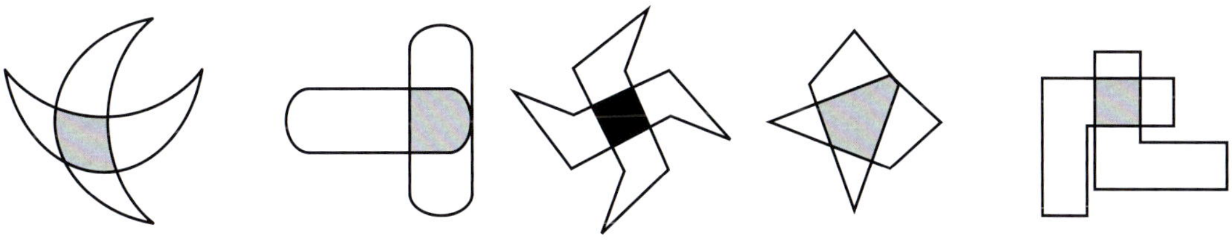

Test Figure   a   b   c   d

Score

Answer ____

3. Level Three

In Non-verbal Reasoning, questions can have three layers:

Test Shape   **Layer 1**   **Layer 2**   **Layer 3**

The Semi-circle has three layers (undergoes three changes):
Layer 1 - It has been rotated 180° or flipped Vertically.
Layer 2 - A Black Filled Bow Tie Shape is added at the top.
Layer 3 - A White Filled Star Shape is added at the top.

Example 1: Which shape completes the second pair of shapes?

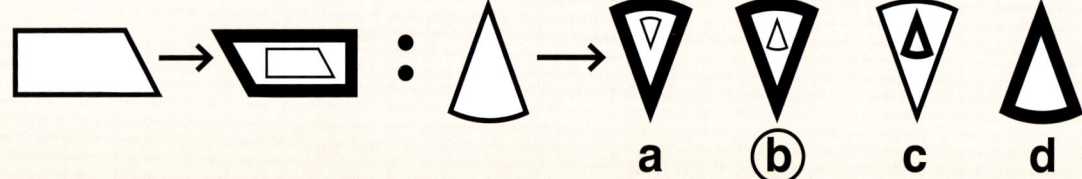

Answer: **b** - The outer shape rotates 180°; the line becomes thicker; a smaller but identical inner shape is enclosed within the outer shape.

Example 2: Which figure is the odd one out?

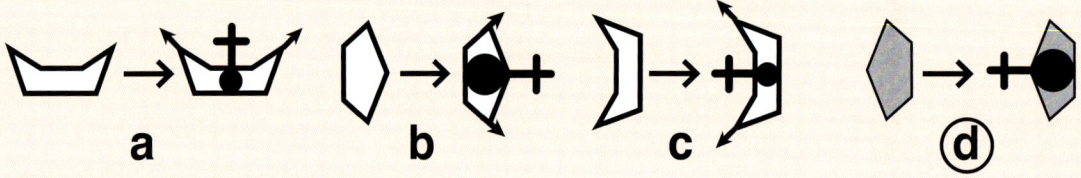

Answer: **d** - The Boat Shape should receive the three additions; **d** has a Circle with a Black Fill and a Black Cross Shape but no Arrow Shapes.

Example 3: Which figure is next in the series?

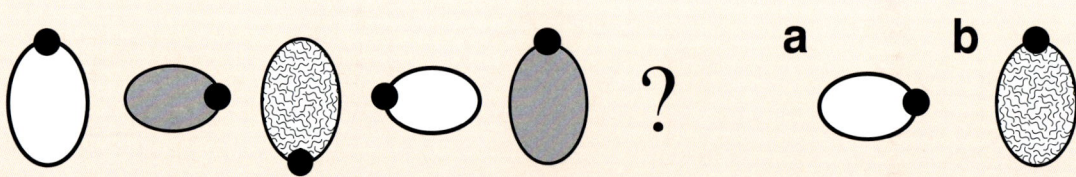

Answer: **c** - It has a Mottled Fill, both shapes rotate 90° Clockwise and the Ellipse reduces in size.

Exercise 5: 3   Answer the following:

1) Which is the next figure in the series?

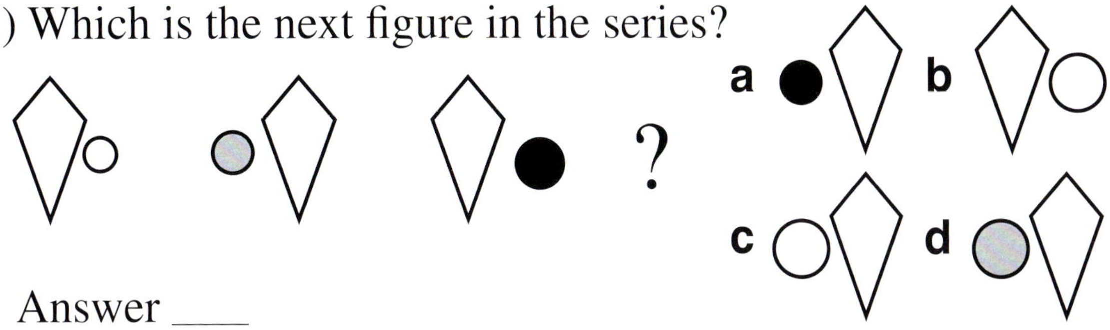

Answer ____

2) Which figure is most similar to the Test Figure?

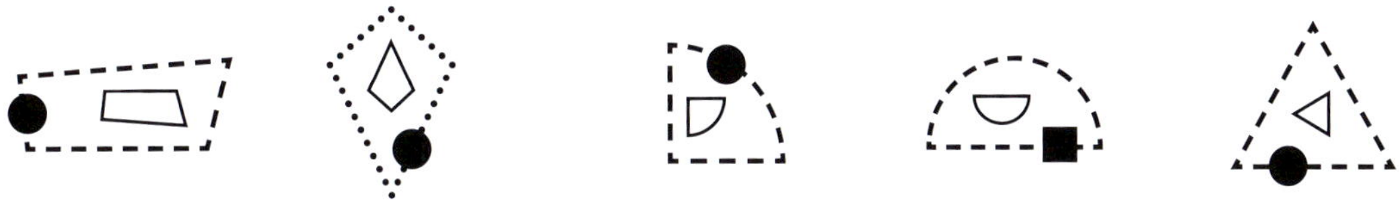

Test Figure   a   b   c   d

Answer ____

3) Which figure is most like the Test Figure?

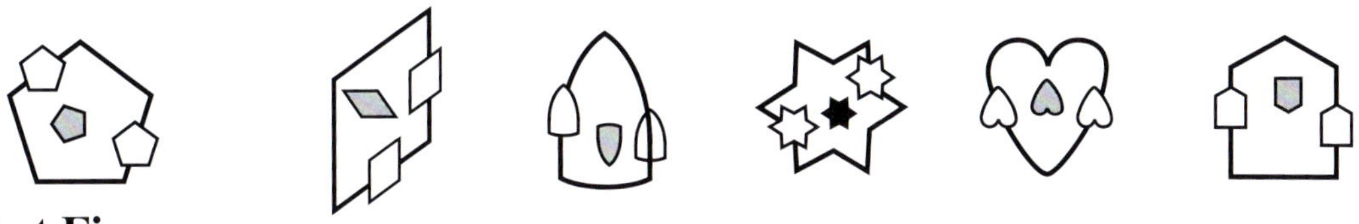

Test Figure   a   b   c   d   e

Answer ____

4) Which figure completes the second pair of figures?

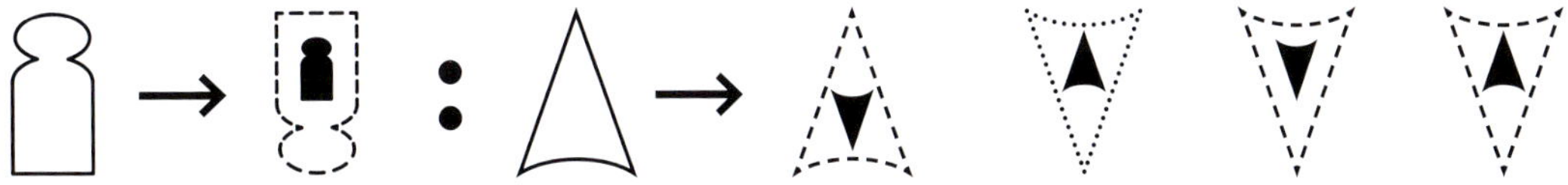

a   b   c   d

Answer ____

5) Which figure is most similar to the Test Figures?

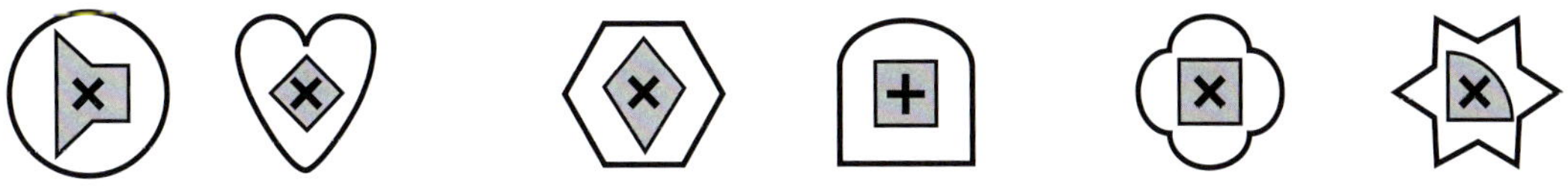

Test Figures   a   b   c   d

Answer ____

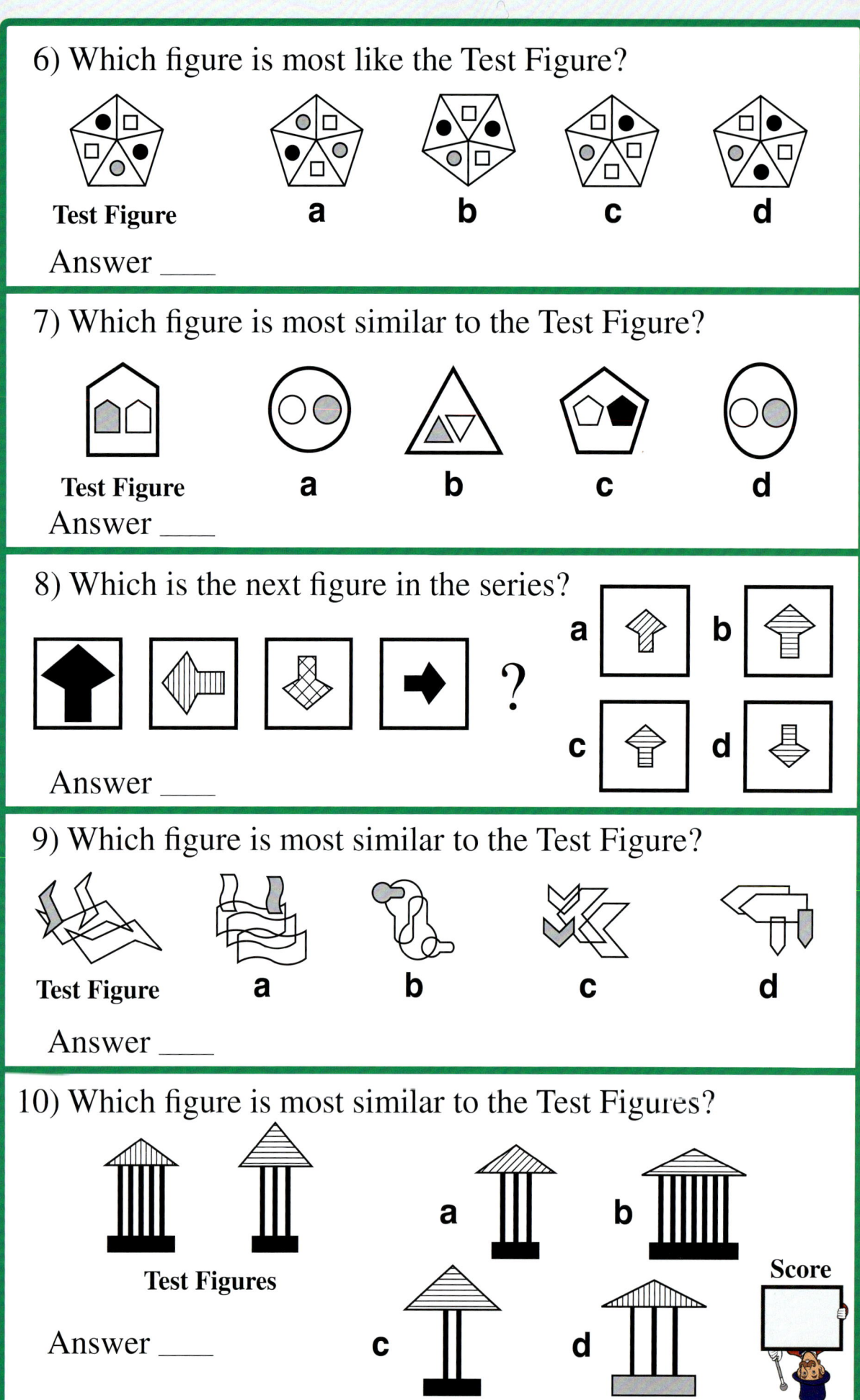

*11+ Non-verbal Reasoning
Year 4/5 Workbook 1*

Answers

Chapter One
Elements
Exercise 1: 1
1) Square
2) Isosceles Triangle
3) Regular Pentagon
4) Circle
5) Semi-circle
6) Equilateral Triangle
7) Trapezium
8) Kite
9) Parallelogram
10) Ellipse

Exercise 1: 2
1) Loaf Shape
2) 4-pointed Star
3) Shield Shape
4) Set Square Shape
5) Moon Shape
6) Straight Arrow
7) Envelope Shape
8) Phone Shape
9) Wheel Shape
10) Bow Tie Shape

Exercise 1: 3
1) **a** - Regular Heptagon
2) **a** - Ellipse
3) **c** - Chevron Shape
4) **b** - Curved Arrow
5) **e** - Cross
6) **a** - Boot Shape
7) **c** - Ellipse
8) **c** - Shield Shape
9) **b** - General Quadrilateral
10) **d** - House Shape

Exercise 1: 4
1) Liquid; Mottled.
2) Shaded; Vertical/Dashed.
3) Dotted; Close.
4) Shaded; Left Slant/Solid.
5) Block; Black.
6) Cross-hatched; Lattice.
7) Shaded; Horizontal/Solid.
8) Liquid; Speckled.
9) Cross-hatched; Squares.
10) Dotted; Spaced.

Exercise 1: 5
1) **d** - Shaded; Horizontal/Solid.
2) **b** - Shaded; Right Slant/Solid.
3) **a** - Cross-hatched; Squares.
4) **e** - Dotted; Spaced.
5) **c** - Liquid; Mottled.
6) **b/d** - Cross-hatched; Lattice.
7) **a** - Block; Black.
8) **d** - Shaded; Vertical/Dashed.
9) **c** - Shaded; Horizontal/Solid.
10) **d** - Block; White.

Exercise 1: 6a
1) Dotted/Straight/Thick; Zigzag.
2) Dashed/Straight/Thin; Cross.
3) Solid/Straight/Thin; Symbol.
4) Dotted/Straight/Thin; Letter.
5) Solid/Straight/Thick; Pitchfork.

Exercise 1: 6b
6) Dotted/Curved/Thin; Fish.
7) Dotted/Curved/Thick; Wave.
8) Solid/Curved/Thick; Symbol.
9) Dashed/Curved/Thin; Basin.
10) Solid/Curved/Thick; Arrow.

Exercise 1: 7
1) **a** - Straight
2) **c** - Curved
3) **d** - Comb
4) **d** - Basin
5) **b** - Straight Arrow
6) **e** - Solid/Straight/Thick
7) **c** - Dashed/Straight/Thick
8) **b** - Solid/Straight/Thick
9) **a** - Symbols
10) **b** - Solid/Curved/Thick

Exercise 1: 8
1) **d** - The Triangle rotates 180° each time and the series order of fills is Black, Grey, White, Grey, Black, Grey, etc.
2) **e** - It is positioned Vertically whereas the others are rotated at 45° or Diagonally.
3) **c** - The fills alternate Liquid/Grey/Dotted and the Quadrant rotates 90° each time.
4) **b** - It is a Straight Shape whereas all the other shapes are Curved.

Answers

5) **a** - The shading rotates 45° anti-clockwise each time and the sides increase by one each time.
6) **a** and **d** - The shapes have Liquid Fills.
7) **b** - It has a White Fill whereas the others have either Black or Grey Fills.
8) **b** - It has four sides like the Test Shape.
9) **c** - The Heart Shape must be smaller with a Vertical Solid Shaded Fill.
10) **d** - It has one order of rotation.

Chapter Two
Movements
Exercise 2: 1
1) **a** - Shaded/Right Slanted Solid
2) **c** - Curved Arrows
3) **b** - Cross-hatched Lattice
4) **b** - The two enclosed shapes should reflect.
5) **b** - J is the next Letter that has no reflective line of symmetry.
6) **c** and **e** - Both pairs of shapes reflect.
7) **d** - i) The shapes reflect. ii) Bean Shapes
8) **d** - Chevron Shape
9) **b** - Boot Shape
10) **a** - Boat Shape

Exercise 2: 2
1) **c** - 90°; Anticlockwise.
2) **a** - 45°
3) **c** - 90° Clockwise
4) **b** - 180° and 45°
5) **a** - Clockwise
6) **b** - It is not a rotation of the same shape.
7) **a** - The Boot Shape rotates in the same direction.
8) **a** - 90°
9) **c** - 90°; 180°
10) **b** - The Letter Z has rotational symmetry (rotates twice / rotational order of 2 - 180° and 360°).

Exercise 2: 3
1) **d** - Merger
2) **c** - Partial Overlay
3) **a** - Linkage
4) **a** - Enclosure
5) **e** - Overlay
6) **b** - Merger/Linkage
7) **b** - Enclosure
8) **b** - Merger
9) **d** - Overlay
10) **c** - Overlay/Linkage/Enclosure

Exercise 2: 4
1) **a** - Heart Shape: Horizontal; Flower Shape: Vertical; Star: Horizontal.
2) **c** - Pentagon: Vertical; Square: Vertical; Bone Shape: Horizontal.
3) **d** - Star/Crosses/Sector: Horizontal and Vertical.
4) **d** - Horizontal
5) **b** - Circle: Horizontal; Bulb Shape: Vertical.
6) **c** - Arrow: Horizontal; Star: Vertical.
7) **d** - Vertical
8) **b** - Square: Vertical; Pentagon: Horizontal.
9) **a** - Horizontal
10) **c** - Vertical and Horizontal.

Chapter Three
Manipulations
Exercise 3: 1
1) **d** - Reduction
2) **b** - Enlargement
3) **c** - Speaker Shape/reduces Square/enlarges
4) **a** - Enlargement
5) **d** - Enlargement
6) **c** - Reduction
7) **b** - Enlargement
8) **a** - Enlargement
9) **c** - Reduction
10) **b** - Reduction

Exercise 3: 2
1) **d** - Triangle
2) **d** - Pentagons
3) **c** - Flag Shape
4) **a** - Triangle; Black
5) **a** - Two
6) **b** - Cross-hatched Fill
7) **c** - Two
8) **b** - The shape has six sides therefore three Circles (half) should be added instead of two.

Answers

11+ Non-verbal Reasoning Year 4/5 Workbook 1

9) **d** - White/Black/Grey/White
10) **a** - i) The outside shape rotates 180°.
    ii) One side is added to the enclosed shape.
    iii) A Grey Fill is added.

Exercise 3: 3
1) **d** - Quarter/Clockwise
2) **c** - i) The enclosed Circle.
   ii) The fill of the enclosed shape.
3) **c** - i) The outer Circle.
   ii) An enclosed Line.
4) **a** - There should be one less Bar than there are sides on the shape.
5) **b** - Clockwise.
6) **b** and **c** - i) A third of the shape is subtracted.
   ii) The outer shape is subtracted.
7) **d** - One third of the enclosed shapes.
8) **a** - i) The Shaded Fill
   ii) The Arrow
9) **c** - One Triangle with a Black Fill and one Triangle with a White Fill.
10) **b** - i) The Flower Shape
    ii) The smallest Square

Exercise 3: 4
1) **b** - 2, 4, 6, 8, 10
2) **e** - Only three of the enclosed shapes must be the same as the outer shape.
3) **d** - Four
4) **a** - Three
5) **c** - There should be two Square Bar Ends and two Circle Bar Ends.
6) **d** - The Cross Shape should have two Grey Fill areas.
7) **c** - There shoud be five enclosed shapes.
8) **a** - Three Black and five Grey Stars.
9) **d** - 1, 2, 3, 4, 5, 6
10) **b** - The sides of the shapes must add up to 12.

Chapter Four
Patterns
Exercise 4: 1
1) **d** - 5, 4, 3, 4, 5
2) **c** - Clockwise
3) **b** - Reflection
4) **a** - White/Dotted/Cross-hatched/Grey/Right Slanted Solid Shaded
5) **c** - Right Slanted Dashed Shaded
6) **a** - 3, 2, 1, 2, 3
7) **d** - Black Square
8) **c** - Grey/White/Black/Grey/White/Black, etc.
9) **c** - Small, large, medium, etc.
10) **b** - Heart Shape rotates Clockwise; Speaker Shape reflects along the vertical axis.

Exercise 4: 2
1) **d** - The outside shape must be an Irregular Pentagon; there should be six Crosses; the Crosses must be rotated 45°.
2) **a** - Dotted, Straight and Thick; Solid, Straight and Thin.
3) **a** - 5-pointed Star
4) **b** - Pentagon
5) **c** - A Line and a Circle.
6) **a** - The outer shape must have five sides and a Black Fill and the enclosed Circle must have a White Fill.
7) **d** - i) Outside Solid Line gets thinner.
   ii) Each Square is divided by four at each stage.
8) **c** - One Flower Shape and one Heart Shape alternatively.
9) **b** - A House Shape.
10) **b** - Squares fill sequence: Thin Dotted; Thick Solid; Thin Dashed; Cumulative action: Circle enlarges, Chevron Shape reduces.

Chapter Five
Layering
Exercise 5: 1
1) **d** - The shape is stretched.
2) **e** - The fill is not Vertical Shaded.

11+ Non-verbal Reasoning Year 4/5 Workbook 1

Answers

3) **c** - The shape has a Thick Outline.
4) **c** - The figure has an Arrowhead line ending.
5) **b** - It is not a rotation of the other shapes.
6) **c** - There is not an enclosed Circle with a White Fill.
7) **a** - The enclosed shape is identical to the outer shape.
8) **e** - The Cross does not have a Grey Fill and the Square does not have a White Fill.
9) **b** - The fills rotate one position clockwise.
10) **c** - The central shape links the other two shapes.

Exercise 5: 2

1) **c** - The Cross rotates 45°. The Star moves clockwise around the Cross.
2) **a** - The enclosed shape has a vertical line of symmetry. The Square has a Slant Shaded Fill.
3) **b** - The number of Arrows is: 4, 3, 2, 1. The Arrows rotate 90° anticlockwise.
4) **d** - The figure is Straight. From the outside, line types are: Solid, Dotted, Dashed.
5) **b** - The number of shapes is: 1, 1, 2, 2, 3. The shapes' positions alternate between left and right.
6) **b** and **c** - The figures are both Straight. The number of sides totals nine.
7) **a** - The Rectangles are Grey and White. The opposite Speaker Shapes have the same fills.
8) **b** - Both shapes are Curved. The enclosed shape is a 90° clockwise rotation of the outer shape.
9) **d** - The order of line types is: Solid, Dashed, Dotted, Solid, Dashed. The Star moves anticlockwise around the Square.
10) **c** - The two shapes are merged. The merger has a Grey Fill.

Exercise 5: 3

1) **c** - The shapes swap positions. The Circle enlarges. The fill of the Circle is: White, Grey, Black, White.
2) **b** - The outline is Dashed. The Black Circle overlays the large shape. The enclosed shape is a vertical reflection of the large shape.
3) **a** - There are four of the same shape. The enclosed shape has a Grey Fill. Two White Shapes overlay the large shape.
4) **d** - The shape rotates 180°. The outline becomes Dashed. A replica of the shape with a Black Fill is enclosed.
5) **c** - The outer shape is Curved. The enclosed shape is Straight. The Cross is at 45°.
6) **d** - The Pentagon is facing upwards. The order of shapes is: Black Circle, White Square, Black Circle, Grey Circle, White Square.
7) **a** - The enclosed shapes have the same orientation. The enclosed shapes are Grey and White. The outer and enclosed shapes are the same.
8) **c** - The order of fills is: Black, Shaded, Lattice, Black, Shaded. The Arrow reduces. The Arrow rotates 90° anticlockwise.
9) **c** - There are two large and two small shapes. The two large shapes link. One small shape overlays and one small shape links with the same large shape.
10) **b** - The Rectangle has a Black Fill. There is an odd number of Lines. The Triangle fill is Vertical or Horizontal Shaded.

PROGRESS CHARTS

1. ELEMENTS

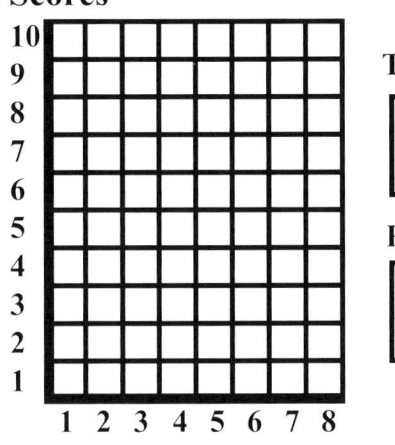

Total Score

Percentage %

2. MOVEMENTS

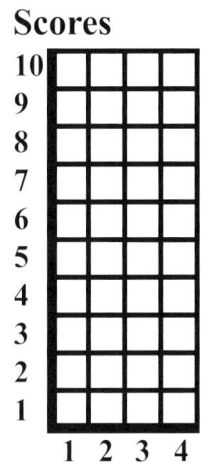

Total Score

Percentage %

3. MANIPULATIONS

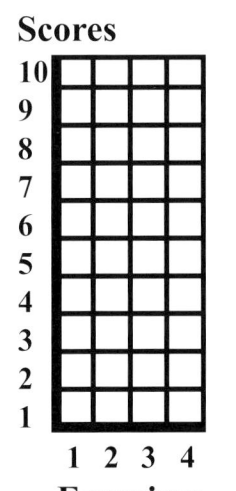

Total Score

Percentage %

4. PATTERNS

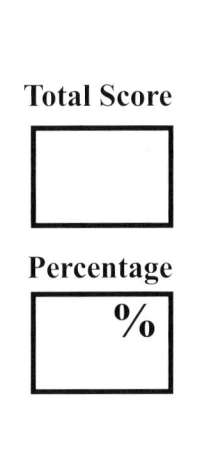

Total Score

Percentage %

5. LAYERING

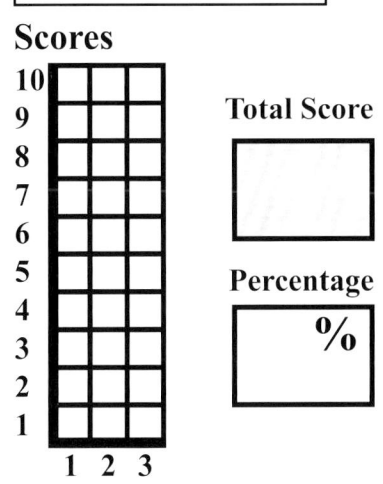

Total Score

Percentage %

Shade in your score for each exercise on the graphs. Add up for your total score.

For the average add up % and divide by 5

Overall Percentage

%

© 2015 Stephen Curran

CERTIFICATE OF
ACHIEVEMENT

This certifies

_____

has successfully completed

11+ Non-verbal Reasoning Year 4/5
WORKBOOK 1

Overall percentage score achieved [ ] %

Comment _____
_____

Signed _____
(teacher/parent/guardian)

Date _____